Hope
for
Hurting Singles

A Christian Guide to
Overcoming Life's Challenges

Jack Zavada

Unless otherwise noted, Scripture quotations taken from the Holy Bible, New International Version® NIV® Copyright © 1973, 1978, 1984, 2011 by Biblica, Inc. ™ Used by permission. All rights reserved worldwide.

ISBN-13: 978-0692884447
ISBN-10: 0692884440

Pine Cone Press
401 Indiana Avenue
Streator, Illinois 61364
U.S.A.

Printed in the United States of America

Table of Contents

~~~~~

How To Use This Book

~~~~~

There *is* hope for hurting singles: solid, realistic hope based on the promises of God.

As you work your way through this book, you'll notice a recurring theme: *"but with God all things are possible."* (Matthew 19:26) In *Hope for Hurting Singles*, we're going to explore how God can help you be more joyful and content, even without a spouse. That's a tall order, but the Creator of the Universe is up to it.

Along the way, we'll bust a few myths, remind you of helpful spiritual truths, and give you some time-tested biblical principles to follow when hard times hit. Above all, this is a book about hope. My job is to make sure you come away with plenty of hope.

I am not a psychologist or minister. My experience with singleness comes from over 45 years of being a single adult. I have read just about every book I could find on the subject, and frankly, many of them were lousy. Just so you know, this book does *not* contain dating advice. You can get that in other places. Within these pages you'll learn real-world strategies for dealing with life's grittiest problems. I've handled some of those well but messed up with others. I'll share both my mistakes and the positive lessons I've picked up over the years. My goal is to keep things practical and down-to-earth.

You'll be hearing a lot about our culture and how strongly it influences you. Maybe you haven't considered it, but we are all products of the TV shows and commercials, magazines, newspapers, movies, web sites, and even music we come in contact with. Over the years, these messages build up. The result is subtle but unmistakable. As a Christian, you may think your main influence is the Bible, but the Bible is not hammered away at you every waking moment, as these other authorities are. While you're being programmed to buy, act, and think the world's way, we'll show you how important it is to keep coming back to the Bible, so you can take stock and challenge that programming with the indisputable truth of Scripture.

Please read *Hope for Hurting Singles* with an open mind. Some of the ideas you encounter here may be new to you. Others may be familiar but perhaps you dismissed them years ago and need to rethink your viewpoint. Remember, too, that our God sees things from an eternal perspective. This life is not all there is. While we must make the most of our time on earth, heaven is real. That's where justice will be perfect and where we will live the life we've always dreamed of.

I hope you enjoy Hope for Hurting Singles.

Chapter One
Turn Your Loneliness into Solitude

~~~~~

The whole value of solitude depends upon one's self; it may be a sanctuary or a prison, a haven of repose or a place of punishment, a heaven or a hell, as we ourselves make it.

John Lubbock

Loneliness is painful, so painful sometimes it feels like a physical ache.

If you're a single person, loneliness is your constant companion. It's there when you go to bed and there when you wake up in the morning. When something wonderful happens, you wish you had someone to share it with. When something bad happens and you need someone to bare your soul to, no one is there.

While loneliness exerts a powerful influence over us, I strongly believe it can be *managed*, to the point that like a physical illness such as diabetes, it's always present but not controlling you. By following the right regimen, you can minimize harmful outcomes of living by yourself and enjoy a normal life. Managing loneliness is not easy, but it can be done.

There are three keys to managing loneliness: cultivating solitude in your life, reaching out to others, and developing an intimate relationship with God.

Too many of us take a passive approach to loneliness, hoping it will somehow go away on its own. It doesn't. Only by following these three steps and taking a proactive approach can we get a handle on it. For reasons I'll discuss later, I do not feel loneliness can be eliminated, but I do think it's possible to be single and happy if you view this problem with an optimistic perspective. No matter how frustrated you have been in the past, it's time to build new hope.

This is not the kind of counterfeit hope that comes from putting on a brave front. Even nonbelievers can do that. No, this is genuine hope based on the principles of Scripture and the promises of God. If anyone lived a hope-filled life, it was our Savior, Jesus Christ. He was single, like you and me. How did he handle loneliness?

If you read the gospels closely, I think you'll find he followed the three steps outlined above. Jesus made wise use of solitude. He reached out to others and made many friends while on earth. Finally, Jesus maintained an intimate relationship with his Father and the Holy Spirit.

By following Jesus' example, you and I can take on loneliness and win. In the end, all forces must bow to the power of God. When we enlist God's help in this fight, we will gain new confidence and true hope.

How to Cultivate Solitude

An inescapable truth of being single is you have to spend time alone. Some people identify being alone with loneliness, but that doesn't necessarily have to follow. It takes courage to dig into *why* you think that way, but learning the truth opens the way to change.

You'd be surprised to learn how much of your loneliness comes from unrealistic expectations. Our culture is obsessed with happiness and having fun. When we're not having fun, we instinctively think there's something wrong with us, and when we're feeling lonely, we panic and believe something terrible will happen if we don't put a stop to it *immediately*.

Being alone and *hating* it is loneliness. Being alone and *liking* it is solitude, and there's a world of difference.

Let's see if we can't turn that around. Let's try, in this section, to learn how to actually *enjoy* time alone. Enjoying it means turning it into solitude. The first requirement? You have to love yourself. Many single people don't. They can't stand being alone because their own critical thoughts attack them, and they become their own worst enemy.

Think about your life. Do you always have to have some kind of noise going on? Do you turn on the TV, radio, or MP3 player as soon as you get home? Are you on your cell phone for hours during the evening? Does silence make you nervous? When you insist on noise all the time, you're trying to drown something out. You may be running away from yourself. If you don't love yourself and don't want to deal with that problem, you may be doing whatever you can to avoid confronting it.

Jesus commanded his followers to love God and to *"Love your neighbor as yourself."* (Luke 10:27)

Most of us miss that "love yourself" part of the command. To appreciate solitude, you simply *must* love yourself and look forward to spending time alone.

How do you do that when you hate yourself or, at best, find your own company barely tolerable? It begins with knowing you are fully and unconditionally loved by God. We'll discuss self-esteem in Chapter Five, but for now let's concentrate on those negative thoughts you have when you're alone.

Are you like me? Do you spend a lot of your thought-life replaying situations and thinking about what you *should* have done or *should* have said? Do you even invent imaginary conversations where you defend yourself or make a snappy comeback to some cutting remark? Lots of singles do that.

Or maybe you mentally beat yourself up, turning yourself into a human punching bag over some dumb thing you said or did. That's much more common than you think too.

Many singles struggle with feelings of inferiority, going back to when they were children. They feel they don't measure up to others' expectations and never will. When they're alone those feelings come to the surface.

I could go on and on about painful thoughts and the way we punish ourselves with them, but the bottom line is that our mind slips into these torturous feelings whenever we're alone and understandably, we don't like it. The most common defense is to have some sort of external distraction going that drowns those thoughts out. Or even worse, we avoid being alone.

That explains why millions of singles (not you, I hope) would rather be in a *bad* relationship than no relationship at all, because they just can't stand to be alone with themselves. For some people, putting up with abuse is preferable to loneliness.

If the prospect of being alone frightens you, remember that enjoying solitude is a *learned* skill. For most of us it doesn't come naturally. Most people watch television or read a book to pass time. There's nothing wrong with that, as long as you don't overdo it. Hobbies are also a constructive way to occupy your time because they teach you new things and give you a chance to explore something you enjoy, as opposed to your job, which you may not like.

Today, many young people spend all their spare time hanging out with their friends. Take it from a person who is 64 years old as I write this: You will *not* be able to call up a gang of friends to hang out with for the rest of your life. Circumstances change. The friends you have now will get married (I hope you will too!), some will move away to new jobs, others will just drop out of the picture.

When you're a young person, in your twenties or even thirties, solitude seems like a punishment, but as you grow older and more confident of yourself, you will find that time alone can be some of the most valuable periods of your life. Only by reflecting and praying do we learn important truths about ourselves, and you can't reflect and pray in a crowd. Don't get me wrong. I'm not a religious fanatic who believes you should spend all your spare time praying. I do, however, think it provides a good opportunity to get closer to God.

Learning to appreciate solitude is an invaluable skill which will serve you well the rest of your life, while keeping you out of untold trouble. Instead of dealing with your destructive thoughts by using drugs or alcohol, it's more kind to yourself to face your problems and work them out. Sometimes singles need professional help to do that. That's all right. It's money well spent.

Solitude, rather than being a curse, can be a great source of hope for you. **One of the most important sources of hope for singles is to have something to look forward to.** If you look forward to your time alone instead of dreading it, you'll start to plan things you can do with your me-time.

A new hobby started during your time alone can turn into a source of endless fascination and can also introduce you to new people who have the same interest as you. Resources are available through public libraries, the Internet, and off-campus classes for you to become an expert in almost any area you choose. You can learn at your own pace. You can email authorities in the field with your questions. You can turn being alone into a time of growth.

I have a single friend who is glad to have her home to herself in the evening. She leaves the ringing phones of the office behind, has a leisurely dinner, then relaxes from her stressful job. She sees plenty of people during the work day. It's a pleasure for her to be alone.

While solitude can be helpful, isolation can be deadly. There's an important difference. With isolation, you become a virtual hermit, hiding out in your house or apartment, rarely going out, shunning the company of others. Isolating yourself is self-imposed loneliness.

Nothing creates weirdness more than spending *too much* time alone. Singles have to arrive at a healthy balance. Obsess over your pet theories in isolation and you risk becoming a crackpot, one of those frightening arguers who thinks he or she is right and everybody else is wrong. If you don't talk with others on a regular basis and get out in the world at least a bit, your opinions become petrified. You imagine others to be a threat. You turn into an old curmudgeon, no matter what your age.

So what constitutes healthy solitude and what degenerates into dangerous isolation? It varies from person to person, but balance is always the key. "Goers" might spend at least one evening or afternoon a week at home, and "stay-at-home" types might spend at least one evening or afternoon a week out. For the shy person, going places and talking to people reduces loneliness. It forces you to interact with others, even if you're afraid. More on that later.

Remember, hope comes not just from praying and waiting, but from *doing*. Learn how to enjoy solitude and you overcome a major cause of loneliness in your life. If this is an area that gives you trouble, you may be tempted to give up before you even try, but you are much smarter, stronger, and resilient than you give yourself credit for. And, of course, God is always willing to help you grow. Getting the edge on solitude may take you out of your comfort zone, but I can assure you the effort and temporary anxiety will be well worth it.

Reject the prevailing belief that being alone is a bad thing. Until and unless you get married, you will be *forced* to spend time alone. If you can learn to love yourself, be comfortable in your own company and look forward to solitude, you will find those abilities invaluable assets in helping you achieve your goals.

If you don't have goals right now, you need to get some! Goals give you a reason to get up in the morning. They help you focus your energy instead of wasting it on worthless pursuits. They fill your time with worthwhile activities. Goals can also help you move into a better job where you'll earn more money and feel more fulfilled. Solitude gives you time to work on your goals. During that me-time, you'll be able to increase your knowledge base and develop your talents. In addition, you can monitor your progress and make adjustments.

Without a spouse, we singles have a tendency to drift. It can be hard to motivate yourself. Achieving your goals will make you feel better about yourself, which in turn makes you more attractive to the opposite sex.

As you work to turn your alone time into solitude--and it *is* hard work at first--you may be tempted to slip back into your old ways of coping, like drowning out the silence or phoning your friends. It's easy to rationalize that you need a "break." Try to resist. Whenever you do something difficult, a little voice inside you says, *This is too hard. You can't do this. Just give up and move on to something more fun.*

Remember that solitude pays precious rewards. You *know* you're going to be faced with alone time. No single can avoid that. Don't fall for the cultural message that you have to be staring at a screen or tuned into something all the time. You're learning a new skill. You're building for your future. You're training yourself to be a more independent person.

One of the hallmarks of maturity is not being a herd animal. The more you think for yourself, the less you mindlessly follow the crowd, the richer your life will be. We say we value independence yet worry about what our friends think of us. We try to impress complete strangers. Part of the pleasure of being your own person comes from the support God gives you. God wants you to make wise decisions, and those don't always agree with the latest trends. As someone who has been around a long time, I can tell you with conviction you can't always trust what is popular, but you can always trust God.

We rarely stand still in life. We are either moving closer to God or backsliding away from him. Yes, you may not be doing anything sinful in your spare time, but is it leading closer to the greatest power and love in your life? Solitude doesn't necessarily have to be about God every time you're alone, but it does give you an opportunity to draw near to him.

The Christian life is about choices. Should I do this or that? When you look at the big picture, every action influences who you are becoming. Whether you understand it or not, you are building character. What type of character you have twenty or thirty years from now depends on what you do today, tomorrow, and every day. Build good habits and you build good character. Follow Christ and you become more Christlike. Making wise use of solitude puts you on the path as a person God can teach. As I said earlier, we can rarely pray or meditate in the middle of a crowd, and the same goes for hearing from God.

God doesn't shout. He won't try to compete with your iPod or television. It's only when you make yourself available to him that you'll hear from him. He decides how he talks to you, whether through the pages of the Bible or through that inner prompting of the Holy Spirit, but know this: You stand a better chance of hearing from God in your solitude. Don't spoil that opportunity. Be receptive to his voice. He has important things to tell you.

Reaching Out to Others

Reaching out to others is one of the surest ways to manage loneliness. When you are genuinely kind and caring, people can't help but be attracted to you. God's wisdom shines through in the command to love others as you love yourself. If you love others and are consistent about it, you will find a lot less loneliness in your life.

You can shuffle through life putting up your own personal force field around you, a barrier that keeps other people from getting through, but you close off opportunities when you do that. Certainly it's smart to protect yourself from the predators of this world, but it's just as smart not to become overprotective.

When Jesus gave the command to love others as ourselves, he knew it would be hard. Instead of loving others, we have a natural tendency to pick at them. While that may temporarily make us feel superior, it devalues the other person. In our own pain, we push away the very people who could help us. And we could help them, too.

To love others, you have to be aware of your own faults. When you rightfully recognize your own sinful nature, you can understand why others behave the way they do. If you're honest, you have to admit you have enough flaws of your own to work on first before you point out the faults of others. That's what Jesus meant when he said to take the plank out of your own eye before trying to get the speck out of your neighbor's eye. A kind person tries to live by the Golden Rule: *Do to others as you would have them do to you.* (Matthew 7:12)

One of the good things about Millennials is they are not as xenophobic as earlier generations, that is, afraid of people who are different. Today's young people tend to take others as they are, not judging because a person has unfamiliar customs or tastes. Sometimes this tolerance goes too far when it overlooks sin, but it has also eliminated a lot of prejudice.

To have friends who will relieve your loneliness, you simply *must* be willing to accept their faults. But let's be clear. You can't do that as an act of condescension, as if you're a superior person doing a favor for an inferior. No, we're *all* struggling. You are obligated to accept others because Christ has accepted *you*, warts and all.

One of the causes of loneliness has always been fear: fear of getting involved, fear the other person will turn out to be clingy or controlling, fear of stepping out of your comfortable routine. As singles, we tend to get into a rut. We prefer the familiar misery of loneliness to the unfamiliar misery of reaching out.

Overcoming any type of fear calls for trust in God. You have to be dependent on his strength, his power, and his wisdom. Even at that, you're going to make mistakes and suffer rejection because other people have free will and God doesn't control them like robots. When you reach out to others, you always risk getting hurt.

Unfortunately, those of us who are the most sensitive worry the most about being hurt. Thick-skinned singles who go charging through life pay as much attention to rejection as a rhinoceros shot by a BB gun.

Completely changing your personality so nothing bothers you is hardly a more desirable option. Again, you have to trust God for the courage to reach out then trust him for healing if things don't go the way you hoped. The other choice, however, doing nothing, is simply more of the same.

We pick up some bad habits along the way that are hard to break. High schools are notorious for fostering cliques that snub others. It seems cute and fun when you're 16 years old, but if you're 35, it's time to grow up and stop it. If you happen to be among the fortunate few who are physically attractive, then people who are plain, overweight, or not model-like in their appearance become easy targets. You may think you've escaped a high school mentality as you grow older, but thanks to those formative years, it's easy to hold onto habits that should have been chucked when you tossed your mortarboard.

Once you get over the misbelief that God is going to answer your prayers by dropping the perfect spouse or friend on your doorstep, you're ready to make some real progress. If you ask God for courage, you can be sure you'll receive it, because courage is needed to reach out in friendship.

When it comes to friendships, new challenges and stepping out in faith, we all need some help. Jesus reminds you that with his love behind you, you can be yourself. You don't need to put on a front, because no matter what happens, his love for you is honest and constant. He loves you for who you are and continues to love you whether you're up or down.

You long for the kind of intimacy and sharing only marriage can bring, but until that spouse comes along, you need friends. Often your relatives--siblings or cousins--can be trusted friends, but if you live away from your family, you need to reach out, *carefully*, and build a couple close relationships. Without them, you risk viewing the world through your own out-of-focus glasses. You can get too used to seeing things from your own limited perspective.

A good friend provides balance. He or she can gently tell you when you're overreacting in a situation. We singles tend to replay conversations from work over and over until we obsess about them. Then we view everything from our own perspective, rarely conceding we might have been wrong. A friend provides needed objectivity.

It's no secret that it's harder to make friends and keep them today. As adults, we've all been hurt, so we become defensive. We don't share too much. We withhold our trust. We exercise caution in what has become a sometimes dangerous society, and that's wise. I don't want to become pals with a stalker any more than you do.

As a man, I realize men don't confide in each other as openly as women do. It's not considered masculine to talk about your feelings. Even when it's done in a joking manner, the other guy can become uncomfortable. I have been fortunate to have some female friends I can confide in. I'm always amazed at their intuition and how well they're able to read people. They give me a perspective I need.

As you're traveling along in life, trying to find that special someone along the way, your friends are oases on your journey. They sustain you and keep you sane. You may expect too much from them and at the same time don't want to give them too much of yourself, but at the end of the day, a kindred spirit, whether a male or female friend, can be invaluable in rescuing you from loneliness. In gratitude you can only do your best to give them the support they need as well. An unequal friendship is doomed to resentment, just like a marriage in which one partner contributes too much and the other hardly anything.

Most women have such a friend. We men, well, we're still too stuck in the world of macho to realize how important such a relationship is. Many men, even when they get married, still hold back, as if revealing their hurts and desires will give their wife a weapon to stab them in the back. As a man, I know it's crazy, but that's the way many of us are. So if you're a man reading this, even if you're not going to tell your best buddy all your deepest, darkest secrets, do use him for a sounding board from time to time. It will help with your loneliness and keep you sane.

Developing Intimacy with God

Deep inside, we each feel out of place here because earth is not our true home. We are aliens in the truest sense of the word. We don't belong here. We belong with God, in heaven.

The wise church father Augustine expressed it well when he said of God, "Thou hast made us for thyself, and our hearts are restless until they find their rest in thee."

A spouse can't solve that problem. You can't solve it yourself, even if you do recognize what's wrong. To bank on your loneliness being cured on earth is hoping for too much. You can do much to *relieve* the condition, but it never truly departs from you. Loneliness is always in the background, ready to surface to remind you that this life is not final. This place is not ideal. This earth is not your home.

It is both discouraging and encouraging that Jesus Christ often knew loneliness. A close reading of the gospels reveals Jesus often felt like an outsider in the world he co-created. We can speculate whether his loneliness came from being homesick for heaven or as an inescapable part of the human condition, but the truth is probably some of both.

From eternity he had enjoyed a loving union with his Father and the Holy Spirt. On earth, confined to the limitations of a human body, away from the perfection of heaven, he was the only sinless being on an entire planet of sinners. In that way he could not relate to his fellow men, yet when he died on the cross, all humanity's sin, past, present and future, was heaped on him with the additional burden of being cut off from his Father for the first time in eternity. None of us can imagine the loneliness of that awful moment.

Some theologians believe Christ died not from the punishment of crucifixion as much as from a broken heart.

Jesus learned from personal experience that people like to be together. He made human beings for relationships, and he may have been shocked when he became a human himself to know those feelings of longing for others. So Jesus knows firsthand how your loneliness feels. He gets how miserable it can be, along with the kind of emptiness that accompanies it. Hebrews 4:5 tells us how much Jesus is like us:

> *For we do not have a high priest who is unable to empathize with our weaknesses, but we have one who has been tempted in every way, just as we are—yet he did not sin.* (Hebrews 4:5)

Let's be clear that loneliness is not sin. Christ is able to empathize with your weakness of being lonely. That means he knows what it's like and that loving you deeply, he wants to relieve your pain. Even better, as God, Jesus has the omnipotent power to heal you of this condition. He knows something must be done, he knows exactly what to do, and he has the capability to do it.

Christ stands ready to help you on two fronts. He can guide you as you reach out to others, and he can supply you with the inner strength to cope with loneliness. It's not exaggerating that some of us need divine intervention when it comes to making friends. Many singles are naturally shy and need the confidence God can supply when it's time to reach out.

In the battle against loneliness, you can do lots of things you thought you couldn't when Christ stands with you. One of Jesus' most-repeated commands was "Don't be afraid." That raises two interesting points: First, he understands that you *are* afraid of many circumstances, and second, he knows something you don't know, namely that you don't have any *reason* to be afraid. When you start to reach out toward new relationships, you imagine you have a hundred things to be afraid of, the chief one being, "What if they don't like me?"

Christ's sustaining power in you gives you the courage to try and the strength to survive if, in fact, they *don't* like you. The thing about suffering a lot of rejection is that it eventually hits you that you're still alive and it *wasn't* the end of the world. You actually build up something of a tolerance toward it, as you do toward hot weather. When you get on a conversational level with Jesus, you might even reach the point where you can tell him, *"Well, that wasn't much fun, Lord, but bring on the next one. I'm not gonna let it get me down."*

When you pray for God's help on those lonely nights, you can rest assured that Jesus is the Master of realistic thinking. Go back to the gospels and see how he always cut right through to the truth of a situation. Yes, loneliness is an unpleasant condition and it's something you'd like to avoid, but the truth, despite your emotions and however Satan tries to convince you otherwise, is Christ is your constant companion, whether you can feel him with you or not.

Building intimacy with God will give you hope. Recognize loneliness as a problem that will be with you all your life, but be confident it doesn't have to be paralyzing. When you experience intimacy with Christ in your lonely times and his support when you're reaching out to others, you'll grasp that loneliness can't defeat you unless you let it. You have learned to control your anger, your impulsiveness, and your fear. With God's help, you can get a handle on loneliness too.

God's presence cuts your troubles down to size. Every problem is puny in the face of his power. That power is yours to receive. If loneliness has crippled you in the past, confront it with new resolve. Remember God is on your side. He stands ready to help, as close as a prayer.

Solitude gives you the chance to develop an intimate relationship with Jesus, and when you do, you have a loving friend you can go to night or day with anything that's bothering you. We singles desperately need Jesus. You don't get to know a human being without spending time with him or her, and the same is true with Jesus. Intimacy with Christ is a gift that must be cultivated slowly, carefully. The way to do that is through prayer, Bible reading, and Christian meditation.

Praying is tough. Most of us don't like to do it. I find it hard because so many of my prayers have not been answered the way I would have liked. In fact, that's among my excuses for not praying:

- I don't know what to say or how to say it.
- My mind wanders.
- I don't hear anything back from God.
- I have other things to think about.
- I find prayer boring.
- I never get what I ask for, so it's a waste of time.

Prayer, in its essence, is talking with God. The key to that definition is the preposition "with." *With*, instead of "to" implies a two-way street. We talk, but we also must listen. I have often been guilty of leaving out the listening part. We all want to hear from God but are discouraged when we don't get that booming voice with a clearly understandable answer.

As you pray to build intimacy with God, you will stumble and fumble. I don't know about you, but the older I get, the shorter my attention span. I'm inarticulate. I can't find the right words to express how I feel. I'm confident, though, that

God already knows. He knows you and me better than we know ourselves, which is comforting.

Give God credit for immense patience when you pray. The One who created you doesn't get angry when your mind wanders or you can't communicate what's bothering you. Scripture assures us the Holy Spirit takes our clumsy prayers and makes them acceptable to our heavenly Father. I think God looks more on the desires of our hearts than he does on our vocabulary. Radio preachers may be able to fashion beautiful, emotional prayers, but that doesn't mean God values them more than a simple, "Help me" or "Jesus, I need you."

To build an intimate relationship with God through prayer demands you be more forgiving of yourself. Over the years, I've realized I can't view God as a cosmic critic, holding up number cards like judges at the Olympics, scoring my prayers like they're some kind of athletic performance. At best, prayer is a struggle. We try to organize our thoughts. We try not to be selfish, but we *do* have problems and we *do* need to ask for help. We fight to stay focused. A hundred distractions intrude, interrupting our fragile train of thought. We start again a dozen times.

Does this sound familiar? I hope it's a relief for you to know it's not just you. We *all* battle an overactive mind when we try to pray. The important thing is to not give up. It's especially important not to quit when you don't get the answer you want. I know it's discouraging, but God wants you to persevere. And remember, since he can see the future and he loves you unconditionally, he will always give you what's best for you, even if it doesn't seem that way at the time.

The second way to build intimacy with God is reading the Bible. Some preachers, and many Christian lay people say, "God said to me..." I don't doubt their sincerity, but that has happened to me only once or twice in my life, and when it did, God did not speak in an audible voice; what he said was so short that it was only a word or two of reassurance or guidance, not a long, divine explanation of my circumstances. I think when we're in an emotional state, we can easily *imagine* God speaking to us. I look for my answers from God in the pages of the Bible, and I think it's wise for you to do that too.

For years I struggled to understand the Bible until I bought a good study Bible with extensive footnotes. I started with the **Life Application Study Bible**. The footnotes tell you how to apply biblical principles to your everyday life. To me, that was priceless. For the first time, the Bible came alive. The Holy Spirit continues to speak to you and me individually through Scripture. He uses Bible stories to give us new insight into our own situation. When I read the Bible thoughtfully, God gives me understanding I couldn't get on my own. It's almost like a light bulb going on when I grasp what's happening. That's the Holy Spirit working, not me.

What makes the Bible a timeless book is the characters in it are no different from us. Sure, the incidents may have happened thousands of years ago, but human nature hasn't really changed. People had the same problems then that you and I have today. We don't always pick up on that in our first reading, though. The wonder of the Bible is that while the words stay the same, our *understanding* of them can change, thanks to the Spirit working within us.

Many kinds of Bible reading plans are available. In the back of your Bible you may find a concordance with topics or a suggested reading for various problems. You can find applicable verses to your situation on many web sites.

I am *not* a fan of sticking your finger in the Bible at random and expecting the verse to "speak" to you. That's a gimmick, not God's will for your life. Some books have more to say to you than others, but those featuring strong characters, such as Joseph in Genesis or Moses in Exodus, Peter and Paul in Acts remind you God takes a personal interest in your life. Even if you don't see mind-blowing miracles happening around you, God is working surely, silently, behind the scenes to provide the people and situation you need to help you.

Read your Bible regularly, if only for a few minutes a day. Be sure to do it in silence, with the TV, radio, and MP3 player off! God will not shout to compete with the noise in your life, but he will speak softly when you give him the chance. He rewards those who seek him. Read your Bible with the purpose of developing an intimate relationship with him and he will seek *you* out.

Lastly, the third way to build an intimate relationship with God is through Christian meditation. We tend to make meditation harder than it should be. I like to think of it as quiet time with God. You can reflect on some specific aspect of God's character, such as his mercy or grace, or you can remind yourself that Jesus loves you so much he died on the cross for you. Maybe you can think about some passage you read in the Bible, or something your pastor said in a sermon.

Meditation is a way to focus on truth. Too often our thoughts are wrapped up in demands like *"I've got to have that..."* or *"It'll be awful if..."* or *"They'll think I'm..."* Notice each of those thoughts is centered around "I." True Christian meditation is focused on God, not yourself. When done properly, Christian meditation not only breaks the worry cycle, it gently forces your mind to accept an eternal perspective. There are big questions in life, and God has the answers to them. While you may not get a life-changing theophany during this quiet time, gradually you *will* understand God is in control, he knows what he's doing, and things are going to turn out all right, even though it may seem exactly the opposite.

Christian meditation, opposed to Eastern meditation, does not rely on mantras or repeated words or phrases. Beware of techniques that recommend that; they're only substituting the name of Jesus or "peace" or "love" for Buddhist or Hindu words. In Christian meditation, you *don't* try to put yourself in a trance. What you are trying to do is get a greater understanding and appreciation for God and the things of God. This may seem the same as prayer, but you're not specifically *asking* for anything or *praising* or *worshipping*. You're putting pieces together. Gradually, with the Holy Spirit's help, you're making sense of the puzzle that is your life so you can be a more authentic follower of Jesus.

Christian meditation is God-centered. While some schools advocated "emptying" your mind or heart, that can also lead to your imagination running wild or even demonic influences masquerading as God's voice. The acid test with information gleaned during meditation is: Does it conform to Scripture? A demon isn't going to reinforce your Bible studies. That gets him nowhere. The path to spiritual maturity is illuminated by understanding, and that understanding is supplied only by the Holy Spirit.

Don't feel you have to sit in a chair a certain way or assume some sort of physical position. There is no required posture for Christian meditation, just as there is none for prayer. I meditate while I take walks. Sometimes I think about God's plan for my life. Other times I consider the complexity of God and how he was able to create the Universe by speaking it into existence. I may reflect on the compassion of Christ or his ability to make powerful truths understandable in the simplest of language.

When you meditate on God and the things of God, he steps in and increases your knowledge of him. Sometimes this knowledge is explicit; other times it is just a sense of God's presence and love.

These three ways to build an intimate relationship with God--prayer, Bible reading and Christian meditation--all have one thing in common. They increase your trust in your heavenly Father.

As your trust in God increases, your loneliness diminishes. No longer do you feel cursed or picked upon. When you truly trust God, you realize he is the greatest friend you could ever have. His friendship goes beyond love to *safekeeping*. When you understand you are *safe* in his hands, life takes on new meaning.

Feeling safe in God's presence isn't just reassuring; it's energizing. It gives you the strength to go on. Think about it. God loves you. He is *for* you, on your side more than any human being could ever be. With that kind of reassurance, loneliness loses its power over you. When God is your Guardian, you know deep in your heart everything is going to be all right--maybe not in this life, but certainly in heaven. It's a great comfort to know you'll be vindicated some day.

All of us feel we have been wronged, especially singles. If you have followed God's commands and tried to live a godly life, you have had to make many sacrifices. The Christian life is not an easy one. You have known mockery, injustice, frustration. For the most part, you have struggled through in a world that does not appreciate you.

But God does.

Ahead of you lies vindication. The gift of heaven, of course, will be to spend eternity with Christ, but you will receive other rewards. One of those will be vindication. Vindication means Jesus himself will say, "Well done, good and faithful servant." That will be enough. Those words from his lips will erase all the hurt. They will prove you right. You will know, without doubt, that you did the right thing.

In the meantime, you and I have to manage our loneliness. To understand that it *can* be managed is half the battle. Knowing that takes much of the intimidation out of it. Like the rest of the Christian life, we can't do it on our own. We need God's help, every minute of the day.

Make no mistake. This is a battle, an ongoing battle you will have to wage for the rest of your life. The good news? You get better at it over time. You learn to depend on God more, drawing on his power as you need it. Eventually every unmarried person learns--or should learn--that beating yourself up is not an option. When you choose that route, you play directly into Satan's hands. Recognize that beating yourself up is a choice; it's either that or turning to God for his help.

Loneliness is a two-sided coin. The other side is solitude. A coin can buy positive things or negative things, but the choice is up to the spender. Spend your alone time with God, on the things of God, in ways that will refresh you and make you more Christlike, and you invest wisely.

Cultivate the solitude in your life. Keep working at it until you turn it from something you dread into something you look forward to.

Next we will look at a trait that causes loneliness, ironically a quality of some of the nicest people on Earth.

Chapter Two
Break the Chains of Shyness

~~~~~
=====

*The way you overcome shyness is to become so wrapped up in something that you forget to be afraid.*

*Lady Bird Johnson*

Nearly half of people surveyed in the United States confess to some degree of shyness, according to researcher Phil Zambardo, and it's a good bet many in that group are single.

Shyness can devastate your life. What shy people need is hope and a path out of their problem. Let's be honest and call it a problem because most problems have solutions, whereas challenges may be something you hack away at, with progress being hard to measure.

I'm not a psychologist or counselor, but I am a formerly shy person. I still have echoes of it from time to time, but my self-esteem is so thoroughly grounded in Christ that I don't waste much time worrying what other people think of me. When you feel that way, you don't have much to lose by taking a chance.

You probably struggled through high school like I did. I didn't date, didn't go to proms, and often kept to myself. The bullies and jocks in my high school ensured that my self-esteem was kept pretty low. I did do well in academics, though, and was president of the National Honor Society. The neanderthal athletes knew better than to match wits with me in the classroom. My sarcastic sense of humor could cut them off at the knees. Unfortunately, I usually paid for it later in P.E. class.

Following graduation, I attended an art school in Chicago. Things went better there because there are very few athletes or bullies in art schools. I was accepted by the other cartoonists, made friends, and had a good time in school. I didn't like living in a large city, though, and transferred to a small junior college about 25 miles from my home. After a year there, I transferred again, to Illinois State University, which had about 16,000 students in the early 1970s. I began to overcome my shyness and finally started to date.

My shyness ended when I graduated from college, but not by my choice. I took a job as a newspaper reporter on my hometown newspaper. I had to interview people I didn't know, some of them hostile, and I had to be aggressive in hunting down news. No more shyness.

It was like learning to swim by having someone throw you off a dock. You quickly forget your terror when your life is at stake. You do what you have to do.

While it wasn't life or death for me, there were many tense moments. One of the good things about it was I was so busy trying to meet daily deadlines I didn't have much time for worry. Reporters covered an event, went back to the office and wrote it up as fast as we could type. In those pre-computer days, almost all our writing was done in the office on clattering typewriters, with phones ringing, people shouting, photographers and visitors wandering in and out, all under the pressure of getting our work done by a 1:30 p.m. daily deadline so the press could run on time to get the papers to the young carriers as soon as they got out of school. It was not an environment for shy people, and because I enjoyed working there, I chose the job over my shyness.

# The inward focus of shyness

We Christians don't like to think of ourselves as selfish, but selfishness is at the heart of shyness: an obsessive preoccupation with ourselves.

Listen to some of the worries of a shy person:

"What if I make a fool of myself?"
"I don't know anyone at that party."
"What will they think of my clothes?"
"If I speak to a group of people, I know I'll say something stupid."
"I'm not as attractive as those people."
"I'll get sick if I do that."

When I suffered from shyness, I never realized how I-centered it is. Shy people are overly concerned about what others think of them. It's a closed little world where the emphasis is on self.

Remember, we're all pretty self-centered, shy and outgoing people alike. The difference with shy people is that they worry unnecessarily how others will perceive them.

Want to know the truth? Those other folks are so self-centered they're thinking about *themselves*, not you! It's a rare person who is genuinely concerned about others, and those people tend to think of other people out of kindness, not insecurity. Truthfully, most people see the world through their own perspective. They're thinking about how *they* can get ahead, how *they* can get their fair share, how *they* can get the advantage on their competition.

Even our prayers tend to be self-centered. I know *mine* are, even though I try hard to pray for the needs of others. As I pointed out earlier, advertisers find it to their advantage to cultivate an attitude of selfishness in the public. Wants are turned into needs and people get very pushy about satisfying their needs. Just watch someone try to go ahead in a line and see a fight break out. From road rage to divorce, selfishness is at an all-time high.

If you're shy, then, be aware that your me-focused viewpoint is not unusual. In fact, it's pretty normal. What you want to get away from, however, is the fear or worry element of it. When you accept that other people are not as concerned about your stumbles as you think, you'll make a big step forward. The other truth to keep in mind is the catastrophes you imagine happening exist only in your imagination. In rare instances you may be laughed at. You may even be embarrassed, but you'll survive, as I did.

In the chapter on self-esteem, you'll see why it's crucial to base your worth on your relationship with God rather than your performance. All of us can have an "off" day or make mistakes. I realized long ago many people are more successful than me, but when it's all said and done, God will judge me in the next life not by how much money I made but whether I accepted and loved his Son. The same is true for you.

I suffered from shyness because I put too much value on the opinions of those other people. I tried to please them instead of God. When I learned I didn't have to perform to please God, it put my life in an entirely new perspective. Now I do my best to obey God out of love, not to meet legalistic standards. There's a world of difference.

Yes, it's true you have to please your boss, teachers, and parents, but at some point we have to draw a line and say, "That's it. I can only do the best I can. I'll do my absolute best and stop worrying about being embarrassed by a mistake."

If you haven't noticed yet, the people you're worried about offending are far from perfect. They make plenty of mistakes and do plenty of dumb things. We all do. The ironic part is the less you worry about it, the less nervous you'll be and the fewer mistakes you'll make. Most of us perform more naturally when the pressure is off, especially if that pressure is self-imposed.

Like anything else, introspection is good up to a point, then it becomes obsession. When we worry too much about what others will think of us, we put them in control of our life instead of ourselves. The desires and standards of man can't always be trusted. The standards of God can, because they are motivated by love. Never forget God is on your side. He has work for you to do and shyness gets in the way. Throughout Scripture we read of God and angels commanding people to not be afraid. You can act with boldness--instead of shyness--knowing God is for you. When you live by God's standards and act within his will, you have a right to be bold and to count on his help. The power of God helps you overcome your human shortcomings. If you stumble, and no doubt you will, God is ready to pick you up, dust you off, and strengthen you to try again.

# God deliberately chose a shy person

We usually don't think of Moses as a shy person. If you've ever seen the movie, **The Ten Commandments**, Moses comes across as bold and powerful. But that's only a movie, and it's not scripturally accurate.

After God appeared to Moses in the burning bush, he told Moses he was sending him to Egypt to free the Hebrew slaves. Moses argued that he was not up to the task because he was slow of speech, probably a stutterer. Then God said he would speak through Moses and teach him what to say. Moses' lack of confidence in God came through:

*"O, my Lord, please send someone else."*
*(Exodus 4:13, ESV)*

At that, God got angry with Moses and told him he would send his brother Aaron with him, to do the talking.

Why did God deliberately choose such a shy, uncertain person to free his people? **Because God wanted everyone to be clear that the power came from *God*, and not from Moses.**

So it is with you and me. God will not give you another person to act as your mouthpiece, but he will give you the power to overcome your shyness. For some of us, this seems like a miracle. It does, however, take some work on your part. Despite your desperate prayers, you won't suddenly wake up one day free of shyness.

Most of what you and I do in life does not require God getting the credit for it, as was the case with Moses, but much of it **will** require God's help nonetheless. I have experience in public speaking, yet I still get nervous when I have to do it. A quick prayer beforehand always helps.

Undoubtedly Moses became less shy over time as he stepped into more and more stressful situations. He got to see the power of God working in spectacular ways until he was so confident of it that he acted with boldness during the Egyptian plagues and on the shore of the Red Sea. When you've been right at the center of miracles like that, surely it would change your life.

Don't look for the spectacular as you confront your own shyness, however. Small, positive steps are just as important. In fact, it's easier to let God nudge you along a bit at a time rather than making the giant leap of trying to speak to a room of five thousand people.

When I realized it was **God's** approval I wanted and not that of a bunch of people I didn't even know, I made a fair amount of progress. Later, when I understood I already had God's approval as his adopted child, I stopped trying to earn it. My confidence went up, too.

None of us want to look like fools in front of others, but at the end of the day, people tend to be more forgiving than we think, and most situations are not as crucial as we make them out to be. This performance anxiety behind much of our shyness keeps us worrying what others think rather than helping us focus on the mechanics of what we're doing. It's easier to remember the points you want to make in a speech when you're not stressing over what the audience thinks of you.

It could be, too, that God has chosen you and me for certain tasks specifically so we will overcome our shyness. Shyness holds us back. I know it held me back until I got a job as a reporter, then I no longer had the luxury of being so fragile. I couldn't worry about what people thought about me. I had a job to do. God may be trying to pull you out of your shyness by giving you a job to do also, even though the situation may not be like mine.

Shy, introverted people rarely get much done for the Kingdom or for themselves. When you step out even though you're afraid and nothing disastrous happens, it makes it easier the next time. You're relieved when it's over, but one of your thoughts is, "That wasn't as bad as I thought it would be." Keep focusing on that thought, rather than, "I don't know how I got through that, but I'm never going to do it again." Each situation you get through is like building your "boldness muscles." Put enough of those workouts together and you'll find you have the strength to step out on a regular basis. Even when you stumble, you'll be able to say, "Well, that wasn't good, but it wasn't the end of the world, either. If that's as bad as it gets, I can take that again." Each attempt is a step forward.

Shy people are pushing themselves forward all around you. If there was an anti-perspirant for sweaty palms, it would probably be a best seller. Your advantage is that you have God to support you. You already have his approval. You'll still have it no matter how things come out. That's worth thinking about before you step out in faith.

# How you create your own world

One of the most powerful truths you'll ever encounter is:

**We don't live in the world. We each live in
our own little world we create.**

Over time, thousands of influences, both conscious and subconscious, filter into your mind. They turn you into the person you become. Every criticism from a teacher, every insult you've heard, every scolding by a parent, as well as the compliments and praise you've received, are lodged in your mind.

You also have a **premise** in your head, or more likely several premises. You believe you are a shy person, or a bold person, a retreating person or a confident person. If your premise is you're a shy person, you tend to grab any influence or information which reinforces your premise and add it to the pile of supporting evidence. When you're thinking about your shyness, you can call up several incidents when you failed to step forward. We all tend to strengthen our premise, even when it's not in our best interest.

To make any change in life, you have to question your premise, and that's very hard. For most of your life you've been ignoring any information that contradicts your premise. Oh, you note it and store it, but you may have a hard time even remembering it because you've dismissed it as untrue.

You treat your premise as true even if it's not, because of the influences of your past.

Psychologists have difficulty helping patients change their premise because it's become so ingrained over the years. They've never thought to question it before; they've always accepted it as true. It's a variation of the excuse, "That's just the way I am."

Sometimes a lot of work is involved, but you can change the way you are--or more accurately, the way you **think** you are.

You may have considered yourself a shy person your entire life, based on the way you've acted in the past, along with selective sorting of memories. That doesn't mean you can't question your premise that you're shy.

Think of it this way: Have you ever judged a person then found you were completely wrong about him or her? We all do that. The same is true about ourselves. You are capable of misjudging yourself, especially when it comes to a negative judgment. We don't live in a particularly affirming society. People withhold compliments as if it costs them money every time they say something nice. Maybe it's because we're all a bit insecure and too jealous to tell someone they look good or they did a nice job. The odds are you've heard more criticism than praise over your lifetime. And too, the criticism tends to sting more. We remember hurts.

Maintaining your confidence can seem like a constant battle. Shyness gives you an excuse to go AWOL (absent without leave). Instead of the assertiveness you need to meet new people, shyness gives you a reason to stay home or turn down dates. "Oh, I'm a shy person," you say. Many people accept that as a valid reason to withdraw, as if shyness is an incurable disease.

Keep in mind you have created your interior world, and with God's help, you can re-create it. You'll need God's help for two reasons: First, you'll need courage to question your deep-seated premise, and second, you'll need objectivity to see yourself as God sees you.

As you begin to question your belief that you're a shy person, you'll find it easy to think of reasons why you feel that way. You'll be embarrassed at the opportunities missed and excuses you've made over the years for not stepping out. It's important to remember, though, that shyness is a judgment you've made about yourself. Any judgment you've made about yourself can be changed by replacing it with a better, more accurate judgment. Remember the inner world you created? For some reason, regarding yourself as a shy person served you well in the past. It was easier to be shy than to be assertive. It seemed to avoid stressful situations but actually created another set of stresses of its own. It provided an acceptable excuse when you didn't want to try. And, by saying, "That's just the way I am," it let you off the hook with yourself.

If you want to overcome your shyness--and that's a big IF--you have to replace your premise that you're a shy person. Your new premise, the premise for the rest of your life, is "I'm a bold person and with God's help, I step out after what I want."

Of course, you can't just say it and expect it to come true. I don't believe in New Age affirmations, and neither should you.

Your old premise had a lifetime of support. It's become etched into your inner world like the other aspects of your personality. To change your premise from shyness to boldness, you have to match it with *deeds*.

**Uh-oh.**

There's an old adage about acting the way you feel, but when you're trying to get rid of shyness, your goal is to *feel* the way you *act*. **Act bold, feel bold.** Of course, this will be stressful because you don't feel bold at all. Your old premise, which is hanging on with its claws dug in, says "I'm a shy person and I feel shy." As you take tiny steps, really tiny steps, to reach out, you'll find once you take action, you *do* feel bold. Your bold feeling will be matched to the size of the act: little act, little boldness; big act, big boldness.

When you step out, it's important to say a quick prayer, asking God for courage. Then after you do the deed, thank him for helping you. Your shyness may be so ingrained this seems terrifying for you. I hope it's not, but if that's the case, your faith in God will be key. Know God *always* wants you to see the truth; that's the role of the Holy Spirit in your life. The truth is you are not a shy person but that you have made a judgment *labeling* yourself as a shy person, and that judgment is false. You are a bold person establishing a new premise about yourself, a premise which will serve you well in the rest of your life.

Because this is such a major change, it's wise to proceed slowly and in small steps. I always advise common sense, too. I live in a small town in the Midwest United States where people are naturally friendly, but if you live in a big city, you simply **must** be careful.

A small first step is talking to strangers. As I said, **be careful**, but you can usually tell who it's safe to talk with. You might compliment the person on their clothing, make a comment about the weather, or ask a question about the store you're in. You won't always get a good reaction, so be prepared if you don't. Many people are scared. Some are grouchy. Others think you're going to ask them for money. If they glare or snap at you, reply politely, "I was just making conversation," then turn away.

The next step involves going out with a friend or relative to a new place, somewhere you've always wanted to go but couldn't work up the nerve to visit before. Your companion is your support system, but don't let him or her do all the talking. The object is to rewrite your Shy Person Premise, and you can't do that if you slip back into old habits. Give yourself points for every stranger you talk to. With practice it gets easier.

If you're making progress and want to build on your success, try going alone to somewhere you've never been before. This is a bit more challenging because you'll still have to talk with strangers but you won't have your support system with you. On the plus side, you've been practicing right along, so you've experienced various reactions. You'll know basically what to expect. If things don't go as well as you like, don't let it throw you. Now is not the time for retreat. Forgive yourself and try again. Learn from unsuccessful experiences but don't let them put a damper on your future. If you want to write a new premise as a bold person, you have to develop a thicker skin. Being overly sensitive was the old you, the you that held you back.

You get the picture. The point is to keep stretching yourself, trying things your shy self would have avoided. This is not going to be an instant transformation. You will have anxious feelings, but bit by bit, you're conditioning yourself to overcome them. You're learning calamities don't happen when somebody snubs you or disapproves. You just slough it off and try again. Don't spend time home alone beating yourself up over how terrible it was. That's the old you. The old you wants to hold you back. Don't listen.

Proceed at your own pace, moving on to the next step only when you're comfortable. You may have to keep repeating a step until you're ready to move on, but don't stay there too long. You know the old you had a habit of procrastination and avoidance. You should be a little uncomfortable when you move to the next step, otherwise you're not gaining ground. Only by doing something you're a bit stressed about will you make progress. Once you do it and get past it, you find it wasn't as bad as you expected.

Some singles will be able to work through this stretching exercise without any major problems, but if you find yourself going into a panic attack, something is happening besides normal shyness. Consult a professional. Some conditions are beyond the scope of this book.

# Hope in spite of shyness

We singles tend to fall into routines that are easiest for us. Shyness is one of those. This convenient excuse has worked in the past with friends and family, and it's a handy way to rationalize not trying. It's normal to take the path of least resistance. That's what "not trying" is.

If you can't break free of your shyness, or if you're so caught up in it you don't want to try breaking free, it can push you into depression or resentment. You may be depressed because it seems as if there's no hope for you. You may feel resentment at me right now because you may have the impression I think it's easy to break free. No, I don't think it's easy. I know it's hard, but I'm convinced it's necessary if you want to be a happier person. You simply miss too many opportunities if you label yourself a shy person.

I have rarely done anything worthwhile in my life without God's help. That's one of the secrets of the Christian life it took me too long to learn: God wants us to be dependent on him. He wants you to depend on him in tackling your shyness too.

Remember Gideon, in the book of Judges? His premise about himself was that he was a weakling, but an angel came to him and said, *"The Lord is with you, mighty warrior."* (Judges 6:12) Say what? If an angel told you that, how would you respond? Gideon argued that his clan was the weakest and he was the "least" of his family. That goes beyond shyness to low self-esteem.

Here's what Gideon learned: He would become a mighty warrior because the Lord said, *"I will be with you..."* You and I can do worthwhile things when we know the Lord is with us. That's your hope in the midst of shyness or any other problem. That's what I want you to take away from this book and carry in your heart for the rest of your life.

You can't do this alone. *"Our help is in the name of the LORD, the Maker of heaven and earth,"* says the psalmist (Psalm 124:8). If breaking out of your shyness seems too hard, remember you and God together can do it. But he will require you to step out. Put your faith in him to supply what you don't have.

Shyness is not a hopeless problem. People all over the world are affected by it. Even people who seem bold and confident have confessed they are secretly shy. God does not see you as a shy person. He is ready to make you bold, just as he was ready to turn Gideon into that mighty warrior God saw him as. All he needs is your cooperation.

You can have hope for major changes in yourself if you humbly ask God to make those changes. You can have hope God will give you strength to step out, once you put your faith in him. Most of all, you can have hope that when you stumble, as you almost certainly will, God will remind you every setback is a learning experience, and it's always too soon to quit.

Never forget: God is the God of second, third, and as many chances as you need. Your hope is in the truth that God's desire is to build you up, not tear you down. He wants you to defeat your shyness because then you'll be able to do more mighty works for him.

We're not all cut out to be a Moses or a Gideon, but we are all intended to live up to our potential. One thing all the doers in the Bible had in common is that none of them did it alone. Even Jesus himself said, *"By myself I can do nothing;"* (John 5:30). He relied on his heavenly Father.

Ask God to help to overcome your shyness. His help is available, it's powerful, and it's your best way to victory. God is your source of hope.

# Chapter Three
# Come Back from Rejection

~~~~~
=====

Since God intends to make you like Jesus, he will take you through the same experiences Jesus went through. That includes loneliness, temptation, stress, criticism, rejection, and many other problems.

Rick Warren

Rejection is one of the most painful human experiences, and we've all gone through it, in one form or another.

Along with regret comes the nagging doubt that you could have done something better or differently to prevent the rejection. That kind of second guessing only makes you feel worse.

When you find someone who seems to be a potential mate, your hope soars high. You can't help thinking, "This is the one. This is the one I'm going to spend the rest of my life with." For many of us, the entire point of dating is to find a spouse. Discovering someone worthwhile can feel like the end of an agonizing search.

Then, for whatever reason, the relationship falls apart. One of the partners had different goals or maybe when things got serious, fear of commitment entered the picture. The reason doesn't matter. Your hope, once such a beautiful and energizing thing, is shattered. The pain is so intense you feel like a walking corpse. If you can experience any emotion at all, it's sorrow so strong it seems as if your heart has been torn from your chest.

How do you come back from such a loss? Is it even possible to come back? Do you join the ranks of the walking wounded who give up and drift along for the rest of their lives?

Whether it's the loss of a potential spouse or loss through divorce, your plans for the future are forever changed. What you had hoped for will not come to pass--at least not with that person. To survive, you have to adjust and make new plans.

The problem, of course, is that you're reeling so badly from shock you can't even think straight. You're numb. The truth you held onto was snatched from you, making you afraid to ever trust again.

In this highly emotional state, you're bound to make unwise decisions. It's common for rejected people to jump back into a relationship on the rebound or for divorced people to marry again quickly, often to the same type of person, to try to re-establish their self-esteem. And too, those who got much of their self-confidence from the relationship feel worthless. Jumping into another relationship looks like a way to regain your status.

The result is usually disaster.

Inevitably some well-meaning friend tells you to start dating again, using the worn-out analogy of getting back on the horse that bucked you off. But human relationships are more complicated than riding a horse, and even though it's true your confidence may be shaky, if you're not emotionally ready, it can lead to even more poor decisions.

Coming back from rejection may also be delayed by the unavoidable post-mortem of what caused the breakup in the first place. Our minds have a built-in need to make sense of things, so like all singles, you think too much. You replay countless conversations, imagining what you *should* have said or done. You examine how the other person broke their promises. You try to place blame, preferably on the other person, to exonerate yourself so you can move on with a clean conscience.

Maybe that's healthy. Maybe it's even necessary before you can get on with your life, but usually we overdo it. At a certain point you either conclude the other person is the worst villain on the planet and was completely responsible for the breakup, or even worse, you discover to your horror that *you* were to blame, plunging yourself even deeper into the pit of self-torture.

That doesn't sound like a reason for hope.

It's often been said the cause of all divorces is selfishness. Actually the cause of *all* human disputes is selfishness. One or both parties have only their own interests at heart and refuse to consider the needs of the other. We're all selfish to a degree. When you're in any kind of relationship, it can turn into a tug-of-war in which each side pulls to get what they think is coming to them.

God is *not* punishing you

As Christians, we can be quick to blame God, as contradictory as that sounds. If you believe God is in control and God could have held things together (as you probably prayed), then skewed logic sees God as the guilty party. Many Christians are convinced God exists solely to make them miserable. I know, because I used to be one of them. I saw every disappointment as some sort of punishment from God.

There are two problems with that attitude, though. First, the Bible says over and over that God is a *loving* Father, not a cruel Father. From the Psalms to Jesus' parable of the Prodigal Son, God is described as the pinnacle of compassion.

He loves us more than we love ourselves. The second problem: God does not punish his children. All the punishment we deserve has already been inflicted on Jesus on the cross.

It takes a mature person to see God as your best friend and constant helper, and not someone who enjoys seeing you mess up. Throughout your lifetime, your understanding of God will change, and if you do your homework, it will get closer to the truth. The truth is God is someone we can count on when nothing else makes sense, like life after a breakup.

Losing faith in God because of a breakup is a serious thing but not that unusual. Millions of people who drop out of church never to return still blame God for some tragedy in their life. Unknowingly, they cut themselves off from their greatest source of strength and support. Going through life relying only on other human beings can lead to more disappointment. When you lose faith in God, and you lose faith in people, what do you have left? Yourself? Good luck with that, then.

Getting over rejection takes time, more time than we want, in our instant gratification culture. Physical wounds take time to heal. So do emotional wounds. You can't rush them. Everyone gets better at their own pace. Knowing when you're well again can be tricky. Some of us stall, afraid to re-enter the world and others jump back in too soon, before they're completely healed.

It's probably wiser to take too long rather than get back in too soon, risking a relapse when something goes wrong. Recovering from such a hurtful experience takes a realistic appraisal of your readiness. Expect to be hesitant. Look for anxiety when you get into stressful situations, and most of all, be careful not to overreact to imagined offenses. In a sensitive condition, we tend to overreact to people's comments, both positive and negative.

God is a reliable compass. The unspoken promptings of the Holy Spirit provide a calm, steady guide for the believer coming back from rejection. Boldness will return as you regain your confidence. God forgives you, but you must also forgive yourself. You can't move forward until you learn how to be kind to yourself again. Singles often view mistakes as the end of the world, but God is always ready to help us make a fresh start. The story of Joseph in the Old Testament is a tale of one setback after another, yet Joseph kept his faith in God instead of men, and it was God who finally exalted him.

To come back from rejection, you have to want to. Yes, there's a time to grieve and cry. There's also a time to stop mourning and get on with life. You owe it to yourself to try again. With God's guidance you can still make something good of your life.

The subtle influence of society

Despite the fact that nearly half the adults in the United States are single (never married, divorced, and widowed), you would think we don't exist. American society is as guilty of rejecting singles as it is of rejecting overweight people.

Christian churches are especially guilty of discriminating against singles. Most are still stuck in the Bible command to "Be fruitful and multiply," implying that marriage is God's plan for everyone. If you're single and have been for a long time, your church probably doesn't know what to do with you.

Oh, the mega churches, which have a group for everyone, have singles' groups and divorcee' groups and even widows/widowers groups, but there's a strange irony to such ministries. Too often, to bolster singles' low self-esteem, such groups try to convince their members singleness is a "gift" from God. One feisty single woman told me that when the pastor's wife told this young woman Jesus was her husband, she snapped back, "And what is he if I get married?" Indeed.

Part of the problem is almost without exception, Protestant churches insist on employing married pastors. Apparently the potential for gossip and scandal is just too great to allow a single pastor to serve. Those married ministers seem to develop an instant case of amnesia as soon as they take their wedding vows. They simply forget what it's like to be single.

Have you ever sat in a pew and endured endless sermons about how to heal your marriage? So have I. Have you ever sat in a pew and heard one sermon about how to cope with the loneliness of being single? Neither have I.

It hurts to feel like an outcast in church. In the one place where we should be accepted and loved unconditionally, we're viewed as an oddity, someone to be pitied because we're not in a state of marital bliss. People who should know better treat parents with young children as if they are the ideal Christian, ignoring the struggles singles are going through to stay on the right path.

If you forget that the purpose of church is worshipping God, you may get frustrated enough to quit attending altogether. That's a shame, but I can understand it. Talking to your pastor and explaining the problem to him or her may do some good but more than likely will not. Married pastors, even the most compassionate, seem unable to relate to the problems of single people.

I have always attended church no matter what was going on in my life. Despite mourning, despite depression, despite callous pastors and irrelevant sermons, I have gone to give praise to God, thanking him for his love for me. Many times it was an act of willpower, but I reminded myself it was not about me and not about the pastor.

Ironically, although our culture rationalizes pre-marital and extra-marital sex, it still holds marriage up as the ideal. Much is made of celebrity weddings. Royal weddings are portrayed as romantic fairy tales. At the same time, no one seems to notice the hypocrisy in the notion that there's something wrong with you if you're single and not in a relationship. Cohabiting is seen as more acceptable by society than living alone.

These mixed messages are very confusing. Single Christians do well to remember our pattern for living comes from the Bible and not from television or tabloids. While everyone around us is doing whatever they please, we are held to higher standards. If you let the culture dictate your morals and lifestyle, you're heading down a very slippery slope.

Too many singles fall into the trap of believing they must conform if they want to be cool, sophisticated, hip, in, or whatever the current term is. When you say "no" to sex, alcohol, drugs, or crime you will be rejected by the people trying to entice you. Unless you have strong self-esteem, you'll be sorely tempted to give in so you'll be accepted by the group. We all want to be accepted. The real question is what will it cost you?

Only a moment's thought will show you Christ's values are preferable to society's. Is it better to be honest or dishonest? Pure or promiscuous? Compassionate or manipulative?

We can go through years of misery before we realize the Ten Commandments were written not to restrict us but to keep us out of trouble. How many people in prison do you suppose wish they had obeyed the command, *"You shall not steal?"* How many people with ruined careers or broken marriages wish they had not ignored the command, *"You shall not commit adultery?"*

It's reassuring to remember the people who reject you for not following their lifestyle give no thought to consequences. You can absolutely bet your life this verse will come true:

Do not be deceived: God cannot be mocked. A man reaps what he sows. (Galatians 6:7)

It may not happen right away, it may take years, or it may even happen in the next life, but consequences always follow, just as the dawn follows the night.

So when you do the right thing and are stung with the hurt of rejection, take courage in knowing it's never a mistake to choose God over everything else. Rejection hurts for a season. Bad consequences can last forever.

Trust God in rejection

Trusting God is a challenge from the time you are old enough to reason until the time you draw your last breath. It's doubly hard when you're going through rejection.

For the life of you, you may not be able to see what was wrong with a relationship or job that ended. You may be baffled why you were turned down for a job when you had the exact qualifications and experience they were looking for. When your character is sound and your prayers are not answered the way you want, you may find yourself asking, "God, what are you thinking?"

That was a dilemma I struggled with for decades. Things that seemed so perfect, so right for me were just out of my grasp. I tried to do the right thing. I prayed. Sometimes I literally prayed all night over a job or relationship but got just the *opposite* of what I asked for.

Looking back, I made two mistakes:

I forgot God knows the future, and
I overlooked the truth God does what's best
for me.

Those were hard lessons to learn. Even now, I still don't understand in some instances why God acts the way he does, but I have accepted the fact that it will all make sense in heaven. I have seen the wisdom of the cliche, "Love is blind." I thought a couple women were perfect for me when, in retrospect, marriage to them would have been a disaster. That's not sour grapes; that's reality instead of infatuation. I thought some jobs would have been exciting and fulfilling, when the truth was they would have wasted my life.

While our physical sight fades over time, our spiritual sight grows stronger. We can see things clearer now than we could at the time, when emotion blinded us. The gift of perspective gives us a sharper view in the rearview mirror.

Try to keep these truths in mind the next time you are rejected: God knows the future and God always does what's best for you. Your situation may seem exactly the opposite, but I can tell you these truths are absolutely dependable. It may take years for you to realize you "dodged a bullet," but eventually that insight will come, and when it does, you'll experience such a sense of relief you'll wonder how you ever could have doubted God in the first place.

Trusting God no matter what happens is the hardest part of the Christian life. Rejection is a time of confusion, even despair. Being a somewhat logical fellow, I've tried to reason out why things happened to leave me hurting, and rarely could I find an answer that made sense. My pastor, Rev. John Gutz, says God doesn't make sense. From a human standpoint, he's right. God's wisdom seems like folly to men. God's ways are incomprehensible at times, but God, being in control, is not required to make sense, certainly not by man's standards.

Atheists' answer to the puzzles of life is that there is no God. The Christian's answer is that God is not required to make sense. When we can't figure out why someone rejected us, we forget God has a plan so complex it would leave us baffled even if we knew what it was. Human beings are not robots. You and I have free will and so does the person or persons who reject us, but God, the master of time and circumstance, has an unfathomable way of turning that into something good for us--even if that good doesn't happen in this life.

As I grow older, I have become more convinced that so much of our hurt, including rejection, will be made right in the next life. I have seen too many saints go to the grave without receiving justice, yet I know God is a just God. Your and my stories are not over when we leave this life. They're just beginning.

With our limited perspective, it's a real chore to trust God when you're hurting. Stuck in the now, you can't see the future and your hope in heaven may be dim. But Christ died so we can go to a place where there are no tears and where all wrongs will be made right. Think of the oppressed people of first century Israel, caught under the harsh rule of the Roman Empire and the constant criticism of the legalistic Pharisees. Most of Jesus' disciples were so poor they lived from one day to the next. They suffered from every kind of disease imaginable, with no doctors to help. They hoped for Christ to be a conquering Messiah who would overthrow the Romans and return Palestine to a land of milk and honey.

Instead, he was crucified by the Romans, stamped out as easily as an annoying insect. His eleven apostles suffered the kind of rejection that brings disbelief. Their world was shattered.

Ironically, the women who lived on the fringe of society, the believers who had been rejected by the male-dominated culture, managed to trust. It was to these women the resurrected Savior first revealed himself. And when they went and told the apostles Jesus was alive, they were rejected again!

Resurrection didn't make any more sense than our lives sometimes do. Even though many had seen Lazarus raised from the dead just a short while earlier, most rejected the idea that the same thing could happen to Jesus, who predicted his return himself. When we demand that God make sense, we commit the sin of miniaturizing him so we can control him. God operates by his own set of rules, rules that leave us scratching our head. The entire point of the book of Job is that God is sovereign--in charge--not us, and as Creator and Ruler of the Universe, he has a right to run it as he sees fit. Just as Christ's death appeared to be final, things are not always what they appear.

There's no question rejection hurts. Rejection feels like the finish, but when we trust in God it becomes a detour, not a dead end.

Christ's acceptance outweighs rejection

To find hope after rejection, we singles must train ourselves to understand what really matters.

You can't live in this world and pretend it doesn't matter. It does. You have to make the most of your life while you're here. It's healthy to want the good things in life, like a loving spouse, a family, career success, worthwhile achievements, and a healthy body.

When you are denied those things through rejection or other disappointing circumstances, it's also normal to feel hurt. At that point you have to make an important choice, and you need to be certain it *is* a choice.

Rejection can affect you so powerfully it makes you want to give up, to retreat into a shell where nobody and nothing can hurt you again. If you don't try, you can't be rejected, and if you aren't rejected, you can't get hurt, the logic goes. Well, retreating into a shell may be fine if you're a turtle, but you're a vibrant human being with the needs mentioned above. Retreating into a shell won't get those needs met.

I said earlier I know about rejection, but the events I mentioned haven't been my only rejections. I wrote my first novel, *Rebel Town*, as soon as I graduated from college. I sent it off to Doubleday and got my first rejection. After spending a year and a half in my spare time writing it, that hurt. But because I understood how publishing works, I sent it out again. At the second publishing house, Ace, it was accepted! About two years later it came out in paperback and I held my first published book in my hands. I was off and running!

My second western novel, *The Wolfer*, was published by Ace and so was my third, *Penwhistle's Prize*. They also bought my fourth one, *The Last Lawman*, then that publishing company changed policies and stopped publishing westerns. They switched to all science fiction. I switched to different genres too, but I kept writing novels in the evening after I came home from my full time job.

I started collecting rejections on every book I wrote. Each year I wrote a new novel. After about six years, I got an opportunity to write another western, but I had to do it under a pen name. That novel came out in 1988 under the title *West of the Pecos*, under the pen name James Calder Boone. But I didn't want to write under a pen name, so I turned down the chance to write more books in that series.

Instead, I wrote detective novels, thrillers, mysteries, fantasy, horror, and science fiction. I wrote 18 novels over a period of about 20 years, and all of them were rejected.

Not one of them got published.

Writing a novel is an exhausting process. Many of them take extensive research, then plotting, outlining, and character development, even before the actual writing. I don't have to tell you about being tired when you come home from work. Imagine sitting down to a computer for another couple hours and concentrating with all your might.

As you read this, you might conclude I was: a) stubborn, b) untalented, c) crazy, or d) all of the above. You might also wonder why I endured such emotional punishment for so long and didn't give up. The answer is simple: It was my dream to be a successful novelist.

I still write novels, but now I publish them as Kindle ebooks. Like thousands of other authors, I bypass agents, editors, and all the gatekeepers who keep books from being published. It's an amazing opportunity I've just started to capitalize on. It's too early to tell if I'll succeed, but I believe if people discover my books, I'll find an audience.

Besides the other rejections I told you about earlier, I had to cope with agents and editors saying no to the one thing I wanted to do most in life. How did I keep going in the face of all this rejection?

I focused on my acceptance by Christ.

I don't know how unbelievers do it. Maybe they're just more stubborn than I am, but when rejection knocked me down, I was always certain that in the most important part of my life--my eternal life--I was accepted, loved, sealed, and safe in Jesus Christ.

If you're a believer, you are too. Look, this is an unfair world. People who deserve to succeed don't always make it, and strangely, some people who don't deserve to succeed manage to rise to the top. I can't explain it. It certainly seems to contradict a lot of the Bible, but I've seen it often enough to know it's true, and so have you.

Rejection can demolish your self-esteem if you derive your worth from success, relationships, or anything else on earth. If you trust in people, your employer, or possessions, you'll be let down. Trust in God and your acceptance by Christ and you have something you can never lose. Jesus will never reject you.

When your prayers don't get answered the way you want, you may feel God has abandoned you, but it's just not true. Remember, your story isn't over until you get to heaven. That's where the happy ending happens. That's where you will get every good thing you deserve, and more.

Rejection here on earth knocks you down, but it isn't the end. Like me with my writing, you can suffer one rejection after another and keep going, knowing in your heart God is watching. He's keeping records. He may not give you what you want in this world, but he certainly will in the next. I can't explain why he withholds the things we desire. Maybe they'd be bad for us here. Maybe they would make us arrogant and cold. Maybe if, like unbelievers, we got exactly what we wanted, we'd think we did it ourselves and we wouldn't be dependent on God. And that's what he wants: God wants us to depend, completely and constantly, on him.

So see rejection for what it truly is, a delay and not a denial, a detour and not a dead end. When you get knocked down, turn to the One who accepted you before you were born and will never let you go. No one sees more clearly than Christ, and he sees your infinite worth. You are precious in his sight.

Jesus gave me the strength to try again. I learned from each experience. Every rejected book made me a better writer. Even if I never get another book published, I can't lose what matters most to me: God's love.

When rejection has you feeling at your lowest, remember God has chosen you. He knows your name. He has saved a place for you in his home. He sacrificed his beloved Son so you can live with him forever.

Whatever you have lost, you will regain that and so much more in heaven. That is your hope in the midst of rejection. That's what I learned and what I know to be true for you as well.

Chapter Four
Find Hope in the Midst of Depression

~~~~~
=====

Suffering is a teacher. It taught Jesus (Hebrews 5:8), and it can teach us. But it only truly teaches us as we fix our eyes on Jesus.
Edward T. Welch, Depression:
A Stubborn Darkness

To hear some pastors talk, you would swear they had never read the Bible. They are so far removed from reality that they judge it a sin to be depressed.

Depression goes with the single life like peanut butter goes with jelly. Of course, that doesn't mean any of us go out *looking* for depression. When you're single, depression comes looking for *you*, and like a stubborn parasite, it latches onto you and doesn't want to let go.

The parasite analogy is a good one, because depression is draining. It saps your energy and joy. It turns life from brilliant, eye-popping color to a dismal gray. And like a parasite, it makes you so weak you don't feel like doing anything.

Depression hurts. This intense pain can go from emotional and spiritual misery to physical suffering, resulting in headaches, fatigue, digestive problems, dizziness, and a whole host of other maladies. Depression can be both a cause of illness and a result of illness. It's so common in single people you may be nodding your head right now, all too familiar with everything I've said so far.

When single people hurt, depression is usually in the mix somewhere. Yet despite the widespread nature of depression, there is still a lot of ignorance about it. Christians, especially, have been told many myths about this illness which they believe as fact.

Let's set the record straight. Sometimes depression has a chemical cause, and all the prayer, fasting, and good works in the world will not make it go away. I always advise people who are depressed to tell their doctor. Medication may be necessary, and no, it's *not* a sin to take meds for depression any more than it's a sin to take insulin for diabetes. Although the stigma associated with depression no longer exists in the medical community, it's still quite strong in the Christian community. The old "pull yourself up by your bootstraps" approach is still around, as are pastors who think depression may be caused by demon possession.

You may have heard someone say Christians have nothing to be depressed about; we should be the happiest people on earth. That view ignores the reality that we live in a sinful world, and the consequences of that sin rub off on every person on earth, including Christians. It's like a girl in a bridal gown trying to walk through a coal mine without getting dirty. It's not going to happen.

So don't feel guilty if you're depressed, and don't allow anyone to make you feel guilty. The important thing is to take positive steps to *treat* your depression rather than linger in it. Just like any other illness, the sooner it's gone, the better off you'll be. Go to your doctor and tell him or her exactly how you feel, then ask what needs to be done to treat it. Any competent physician will take you seriously and recommend treatment options.

When you're struggling in the depths of depression, it seems impossible to have any hope, but when you hit bottom, the only way to go is up. The good news? You don't have to climb out of that steep pit of depression by yourself.

The cause of your depression

For many singles, depression can be traced directly to the fact that they are not married and don't foresee that ever happening. They have given up hope they will ever have a spouse to love and be loved by.

In my work with my web site, *www.inspiration-for-singles.com*, I frequently get emails from women in their 30s and 40s saying they are old and will never get married. They have been taught to feel that way because our culture puts such an emphasis on youth. So many television shows feature actors in their 20s that most singles feel ancient on their 30th birthday. And while women are marrying later in life after establishing their career, tradition still puts brides in their 20s, adding to the pressure. Outside America, women may marry much younger, making them feel old in their mid to late 20s!

I'm not belittling these women's feelings. Their feelings are very real. Those feelings, however, are not realistic.

Marriage can happen at any age. When you tell a depressed single that, their first reaction may be to argue that the odds get slimmer the older you get. I'm not sure that's true. Many fine people of all ages are looking to get married. You can probably think of people in their 40s, 50s, or 60s who got married or remarried. This is not a pep talk; it's the truth.

As you grow older, you will come to appreciate the wisdom you pick up only through experience. Minor frustrations no longer become a cause for panic. Life feels less threatening. You gain the perspective to not take yourself so seriously.

Believe it or not, you become a better prospective spouse as you gain a bit of maturity. While it's true you miss the opportunity to "grow up" together, you also miss the fights, arguments and stubbornness over petty differences that, in the long run, really don't matter.

Too often a single person will look at their life and say in a panicky voice, "Nothing's happening! Nothing's happening!"

But life isn't a movie, going from one passionate romance to another. If your life is like that, it's not passion that's running it but shallowness. Too many singles today, including some Christian singles, have a revolving door on their bedroom, as if that's the correct place to audition potential spouses. That goes beyond shallowness into desperation. What you don't see on television or in the movies is that real people have feelings. If you use people and throw them away like an old Kleenex, you're a predator. If you're on the receiving end of being used, you already know how miserable you are without me rubbing it in.

I am assuming, though, that you are a good, sincere person who wants to get into a loving marriage.

In the final analysis, depression is harmful to your life and to finding a mate. You may feel the ship has sailed on the latter, but it could be the negative outlook which accompanies depression has hampered your chances. Depression is both a mental and physical health issue. You simply *must* face it, deal with it, and drive it out of your life. I can't emphasize enough that your doctor is your best ally in doing that.

Only when you climb out of depression will you be able to view your life objectively and gain a constructive attitude toward things. We singles automatically decide our desire for marriage is the big motivating force in our lives, but it could be something else entirely. A mature person can see marriage is not the ultimate solution for all problems. In fact, if you go into marriage with a lot of problems, it's likely they'll get get worse, not better.

The cause of your depression, then, may not be lack of a spouse. It may be lack of recognition or affirmation, lack of career fulfillment, unaddressed frustration or anger over life in general, or low self-esteem. It takes a hard, honest look at your life to get to the bottom of what's really bothering you, and sometimes it takes professional help to dig out the causes of unhappiness. Singles can have tunnel vision when it comes to marriage. Some of us spend so much time daydreaming about it that we assume things which may not be true. Even if you're examining your life when you're not depressed, it may take the objectivity of a trained outsider to tell what's going on.

In my own case, along with maturity came acceptance of my singleness. I can't tell you at what age that happened, but at a certain point it no longer bothered me that I am single, even though it bothered other people that I am. Hey, that's their problem. I wasn't always that way, and I can sympathize with single women who are stung when someone makes a rude remark. It's not that I gave up or decided I was never going to get married, but slowly my mind changed, or more likely God changed it for me, and I began to see the single life was not as bad as I thought. It sounds inconceivable to you now, but there are some aspects of being single which are very enjoyable. I won't go through them; you wouldn't believe me anyway, but many of my single friends in their 50s and 60s are genuinely happy with their lives.

Getting back to the cause of your depression, it may, indeed, be because you are not married. The two extreme responses to that can be desperation or apathy. Some single women sleep around, thinking they can hook a husband that way. As a fisherman, I know you usually land the kind of fish that likes the bait you use. In other words, if you want an intelligent, caring Christian man and you use sex as a bait, it's likely you'll end up with a player instead. And if you're a Christian man looking for a chaste, God-centered spouse, if you use the bait of wealth and materialism, you'll likely end up with a shallow gold-digger. Be careful what bait you use.

Don't forget where your worth lies

The most immobilizing aspect of depression is a feeling of complete worthlessness. Your emotions take over and overrule what you know to be true.

We always underestimate the world's influence on us, but if you pay attention to Scripture, especially Paul's letters, you see the world's expectations and fallenness are constant pressures you can never escape. Add to that your own expectations and those of your family and friends and you find yourself in a situation where you can never measure up. It's easy to get depressed when you believe you have disappointed everyone and yourself.

But the truth we singles must keep coming back to is we cannot disappoint God. No one is more aware of our fallen nature than he is. That is why he sent his Son as our Savior. As much as we may try to live an obedient life, none of us can do it. Not one of us, even you.

When it comes to achievements, accomplishments, or measuring up, you cannot disappoint God either. As a Christian, you are perfect in his eyes through the credited righteousness of his son, Jesus. All of us often forget that.

Whose approval matters most? Parents? Siblings? Friends? Your boss's? Even your own? No. God's approval matters first, most, and forever. When you're caught in the self-punishing depths of depression, all you can see is your shortcomings. All God can see is your preciousness to him.

It does not feel like it to you, but to your Creator you are a child of infinite worth. That is an indisputable fact, revealed in God's own Word. In his eyes, you are beautiful, no matter what others think of you. In his eyes you are a joy. In his eyes you are of such value he gladly sacrificed his beloved Son so he could adopt you into his family, making you an equal heir with Jesus.

When you're depressed, that truth is so easy to forget. Satan would like nothing more than to hold you down and fill you with doubt. God is the exact opposite. His motivation toward you is solely one of perfect love, always looking out for your best interest, always concerned about bringing you home to his heart someday.

From beginning to end, the Bible is filled with one poignant example after another of God loving his people. His love is extravagant, and as a believer, you are caught in it. All your emotions may deny it when you are depressed, but emotions never change the truth. You may not be able to feel his love, but it is there. I have often made the mistake of believing that because I could not feel God's love or because I was going through a crisis that he had abandoned me. I felt alone, and that's how we all feel when we're depressed. As I have matured in my faith, however, I stubbornly refuse to give in to doubts when tragedy hits. Even if I can't pray, I hold on to the truth that God is my hope and my salvation. That's the path for you, too, even if it seems as if God has forgotten you. He hasn't.

I can't explain the silence of God when we're depressed. Some things we'll only understand in heaven. But I do know his silence does not change his love for you. We expect God to act like people do, and it's a good thing for us he doesn't. He doesn't change, like people do. He doesn't pout or get in a bad mood or break off his friendship. He is a God of his word. Once he takes you into his family, you are his child forever, which includes whatever you're going through during this often painful journey on earth.

One of the most profound truths in the Bible is God loved you before you were formed in your mother's womb. When you chose Jesus, an unbreakable contract was sealed. Along with salvation comes such a mighty love it will raise you to eternal life with your Father. A love like that can't be affected by whether we feel it here on earth. It is invincible and it is for you.

What drew crowds to Jesus like pins to a magnet was not his appearance or his voice but the pure love that emanated from him. Compared to human love, it was overwhelming, stunning. In the Old Testament, we are told no man may see God and live. Not only is that because of his perfection, but also because of his tremendous love. We will be able to fully experience a love that strong only in the next life, and yet it exists toward us now.

I can't repeat this often enough: God loves you not for what you do or what you look like but simply because you're you. This is hard to accept when you're depressed. When you feel worthless, you ask, "Who am I? I'm nobody?" You are somebody to God, somebody lovable. When you're depressed, you don't have to do or succeed to gain God's love and acceptance. You already have it, even if you can't feel it.

The answer to "What's the use?"

When you're depressed, you don't want to do anything. You don't have any motivation. You could stare out the window at nothing for hours. People who have never experienced depression might tell you to "get over it" or stop having your "pity party." Self-pity is a scathing accusation people make toward the depressed, but it's usually a misplaced barb born of ignorance. Nobody chooses depression. Depression is pain, and nobody chooses pain.

The "old school" solution might have been to get moving, do something and you'll feel better. Surprisingly, some minor accomplishment like cleaning the house, balancing your checkbook, or doing the laundry actually might make you feel better because it gives you a sense of achievement and momentarily engages your mind, taking it away from depressive thoughts. While we can try to work ourselves into exhaustion or keep ourselves so occupied we can't think of whatever's bothering us, that hectic spurt of activity doesn't work for long. It's a Band-Aid approach to a deeper problem.

Many singles function for years with low-grade depression, going to work, visiting family and friends, even going through the motions at church. If it were not for willpower and the need to pay bills, some of us would not get anything done.

When your thinking is colored by depression, everything seems hopeless. The logic says past attempts didn't work, so "What's the use?" It's easier to sit and stare or just sleep.

Unless you're a single parent, you're in the dilemma of not having anyone relying on you, except maybe a pet. And except for losing your job, there doesn't seem to be much reason to get your life in gear again.

Except that you owe God.

You don't owe God for your salvation, of course. We can't earn it and we can't pay it back, even if we wanted to. None of us is qualified to do that.

No, I'm talking about the responsibility of every Christian to set an example for nonbelievers and family. We preach by our character. When we're depressed, we persevere not for selfish reasons but because our purpose in life is to glorify God and enjoy him forever. Being saved, we should want to see others saved. We possess a great gift to pass on whether we feel like it or not on a given day.

Consider the enormous privilege to lead another person to Christ. That's the answer to the question, "What's the use?"

I'm not talking about going out and evangelizing. I'm talking about putting one foot in front of another until your depression passes and the clouds drift away. If you have been to your doctor and followed his or her advice, your depression will eventually pass and you'll begin to enjoy life again.

Sometimes just living your everyday life can be your way of spreading the gospel. Everyone was not cut out for the mission field. Plenty of opportunities exist here at home and in the workplace. People are watching us, whether we realize it or not. We should give them something worthwhile to watch.

You and I both know we can't just "snap out of it" when we get depressed. That doesn't work. But we can carry on with our duties to the best of our ability, constantly reminding ourselves of God's unfailing love and that eventually, this too will pass.

The greatest heroes of life are not the soldier who captures the enemy, or the firefighter who saves a child, or the athlete who wins the game. The greatest heroes are the brave men and women who put one foot in front of another, honoring their obligations, carrying on despite the invisible arrows flying all about them. The greatest heroes are everyday folks who keep going in spite of their personal afflictions.

You can be one of those heroes. You owe it to yourself and you owe it to God. When you can't find a reason to do anything, remember the gift of your salvation. By continuing in the fight, you show your gratitude to the Almighty and you give yourself a reason for living. In the end, life is not about the wealth, awards, or recognition we gather for ourselves. It's about serving and glorifying God. When your strength is low, maybe the best you can manage is simply doing the task at hand.

Break life down into the task at hand. If it's making dinner, the tasks are setting the table, cooking the meal, clearing the table, then cleaning up the kitchen. When you don't feel like doing anything for yourself, do it for God.

Even if you feel no ambition at all, you can get through the task at hand. Break it down into small steps. Offer each step as a prayer of thanks for what God has done for you in the past and what he certainly will do for you in the future. Congratulate yourself when you complete it. Reward yourself, if you like. Then move on to the next task at hand, knowing you finished the last one, so you are capable of the next one.

Remember: Sometimes the goal is simply to make it to bed time. One task after another. Small steps, broken down. Hour by hour, minute by minute.

There is a purpose to your life whether you can understand it or feel it. That purpose may be as simple as a word of encouragement or a helping hand to someone else who needs it. During depression, the most important lesson God teaches you is compassion. You learn how to identify with others who are hurting. You learn how apply the Golden Rule to them.

Discouragement over "the rut"

We singles can go on for years without a meaningful change in our lives. It's call being in a rut, and even though we know we're in a rut, we can be reluctant to admit it. Married people get in a rut too. It's nothing to be ashamed of. Ruts are comfortable. Ruts can even be reassuring. We know what's going to happen, and even if it's not great, there aren't any stressful changes. We just sort of do the daily grind, not expecting anything better.

There's an old saying worth remembering: "If you always do what you always did, you'll always get what you always got."

After months, sometimes years of being in a rut without relief, some of us look at our future and wonder, "Is this as good as it gets?" Then comes discouragement, and often depression.

Inertia is the biggest enemy of singles, and it's triply hard to get motivated to change when you're depressed. The energy to climb out of a rut just isn't there. That's why it's so crucial to talk to your doctor about your depression. In countless cases, medication or therapy has made all the difference in the world.

When you get in a rut, you have two choices. You can remain there or get out of it. Keep in mind that doing nothing, avoiding making a choice, is a choice in itself. It's important to recognize that. Staying in a rut, or a routine, if you prefer that word, is acceptable to many singles, and you may be one of them. It's simply too traumatic to go out and do new things or meet new people or take the steps you must to climb out. Maybe you did reach out in the past, things didn't work out, and you're too discouraged or depressed to try it again.

Frankly, I can't criticize you if you're satisfied with your routine. Your circumstances may dictate it's the best choice for you, at least for now. Maybe your health or finances or job situation demand you play it safe, and there's nothing wrong with that. We singles hear a lot of advice about taking a risk or jumping in with both feet or whatever it's called now, and sometimes that leads to a bad decision with the consequence of a lot of misery later. The area of sex immediately comes to mind. Unwanted pregnancies, STDs, and even AIDS are the consequences of unsafe decisions. How many people get into hasty marriages because they thought they could straighten the other person out or because they thought it was their last chance?

No, safety has its benefits. In a society addicted to thrills, living a chaste, conservative life may not produce much sensual pleasure, but let's call uninhibited indulgence what it is: sin. You'll never hear the word "sin" used on television or in movies, and you'll never see actors meditating in regret over wrong choices, but it's a daily occurrence in real life.

So if you're depressed over being in an unexciting routine, think for a while about the bad things that could be going on in your life. You may go to bed tonight heaving a great sigh of relief over all the trouble you're avoiding.

The wrong way leads to bad consequences; the right way leads to good consequences. It's good choices vs. bad choices. As a Christian, you have the advantage of the guidance of the Holy Spirit and the Word of God. You can't allow society to dictate how you're going to live your life. That's why so many singles are messed up. They listened to the wrong voices, and there are many voices today and they are nonstop.

In the midst of depression we singles need to pray for the courage to step out, with God's leading. God commanded Joshua to be "strong and very courageous." David told his son Solomon to be "strong and courageous." We need strength and courage to break out of a rut, and I believe God will supply it if we ask him.

Instead of being depressed over your routine, congratulate yourself for obeying God's law. You may stand out from others, you may hear ridicule from your friends or coworkers because of your Christian lifestyle, but recognize the right things you're doing. Take heart in the trouble you have avoided. If and when you get ready to step out and try new things, ask for and expect God's guidance and protection. If your motives are right, you can be sure you will receive it.

Discouragement over your situation can be the motivator you need to help you make changes. Again, grab onto the truth that you are the one who has to start the ball rolling. Dr. Nathaniel Branden, a wise therapist and the author of *The Six Pillars of Self-Esteem* (a book you should definitely read), said he knew his patient had turned the corner when they took responsibility for their own life.

We singles, especially women, need to get over the Disney cartoon philosophy that Prince (or Princess) Charming is coming. Branden is blunt about it: **No one is coming to rescue you.** If you are going to get out of your rut or routine, you're going to have to start things rolling yourself. We Christians can pray and pray for years, treating God like a cartoon genie who's going to drop that perfect person in our lap. When you study the people in the Bible, they usually *did* something. It's wise to wait on God, but we can't use that as an excuse for total inaction.

Find strength in your weakness

The core of the Christian life is depending on God. While most of us accept that we depend entirely on the sacrifice of Jesus for our salvation, we still want to do the rest of it alone. Life consists of a series of painful lessons to convince us otherwise. The more we ignore those lessons, the more God repeats them until we finally catch on. I have been particularly thick in that area and was well into my fifties before the message sunk in.

David was one of many Bible figures who wrestled with depending completely on God. He also suffered from depression, and with good reason. He hit emotional valleys many times, but one of the early episodes was when the Amalekites staged a surprise raid on Ziklag. David and his men were away. The enemy kidnapped all the women and children:

> *"And David was greatly distressed, for the people spoke of stoning him, because all the people were bitter in soul, each for his sons and daughters. But David strengthened himself in the LORD his God." (1 Samuel 30:6, KJV)*

When we find ourselves in the deep pit of depression, the solution for us singles is to strengthen ourselves in the LORD our God.

Because I've been there, I know firsthand how hard it is to pray in times like that. In fact, it may be humanly impossible. Even for our prayer we have to depend on God, in the groanings of the Holy Spirit that fly right up to the throne of the Father.

Maybe the best you can do is just hang on, with only enough strength to get to bed time. But that's enough. In the heart of depression, it's enough to make it one day at a time. God, in his wisdom, may give you only enough strength to make it for that day, just as he gave the Israelites one day's worth of manna at a time. Why? To make them depend on him. To teach them to trust him and him only, day by day.

I took cobalt radiation treatments for cancer when I was 25 years old. They inflicted a devastating toll on my body: vomiting, diarrhea, coughing, dizziness, and immobilizing fatigue. I couldn't stand to look ahead to the next day's treatment and the violent reaction that would come with it. I fell into despair because I was sicker than I had ever been in my life. I couldn't pray, but others were praying for me. God graciously apportioned his strength to me, just enough to get me to bed time. I depended on him like a baby does on its mother. One day at a time I made it through that 55-treatment ordeal.

God does not punish his adopted children. I believe he hurts when such a trauma happens to us, but as I found out in my radiation therapy, sometimes harsh treatments are necessary to produce a cure. I did not resent the doctors who were treating me, and I could not resent God either.

All healing takes time. We would like our depression to stop immediately so we can get on with life, but that may not be God's plan. In the Lord's Prayer, Jesus taught us to ask for our "daily" bread, not our yearly bread. In the same way, we need enough strength to get through today. Jesus warned us not to be anxious about tomorrow because today has enough troubles of its own.

It's hard to be patient when you're depressed. Again, our instant gratification culture wants a magic cure so we can get on with the important work of running our own lives. But that's not how God sees it. He demands we slow down, and if we don't do that by ourselves, he often steps in and brings us to a complete stop.

Depression makes it hard to concentrate. Even if you want to pray and read your Bible, your mind may not cooperate. Honestly, reading your Bible may be the last thing you feel like doing, and even if you force yourself, you may not get much good out of it. I found the radiation scrambled my thinking. When I tried to read, I kept rereading the same paragraph over and over because I couldn't retain it. I had to give up. I couldn't pray either.

Whether you have physical pain, the inability to focus, or just a loss of interest, God understands. He knows what you're going through better than you do. Don't worry. He makes allowances for your human weaknesses. Turn your will toward him, however weak it may feel. He will connect and pour his strength into you in return.

The apostle Paul, a hard-headed man if there ever was one, had to learn the importance of depending on God through trials, the same way we do. After he knew that inpouring of God's strength, he got to the point where he even welcomed trials:

"That is why, for Christ's sake, I delight in weaknesses, in insults, in hardships, in persecutions, in difficulties. For when I am weak, then I am strong." (2 Corinthians 12:10)

I don't know about you, but I don't feel very strong when I am weak. I feel weak. That doesn't mean God isn't working in me as he did in Paul. It probably does mean we can't rely on our feelings as if they are always true. All we need is enough strength to make it to bed time. Remember: day by day.

Throughout your life, you are like one of those three-masted sailing ships you've seen in movies. They look so impressive, yet they depended entirely on wind. Without wind in their sails, they went nowhere. God is the wind in your sails. He never abandons you, but for reasons known only to him, he sometimes seems to withdraw. When you're depressed, you feel like a ship in calm waters. There's no wind. You're not moving. Your life seems at a standstill. But the wind will return, and when it does, you'll feel yourself moving again, traveling across the sea of life to a new destination. You'll understand, anew, the need for complete dependence on God.

Clearly we singles don't think accurately when we're depressed. You see the world and yourself through gray-tinted glasses. Any judgments you make are bound to be slanted in favor of pessimism. It's not a wise time to make any important decisions.

Pessimism affects your sense of hope about getting out of your depression. You overestimate the odds against you. You see a breakout as overwhelming because of your diminished sense of your own capabilities. You perceive yourself to be inadequate even though your abilities are the same as they were before you became depressed.

Well, despite all the logic and truth in the world, you may still choose to believe your emotions, because that's the way depression runs. You feel powerless in its grip. Everything seems too much of an effort and it's easier just to stay where you are. It comes down to the old saying, "Don't confuse me with logic!"

I think you'll agree, however, we take one of three approaches to a problem. First, we can refuse to admit a problem exists. Second, we can acknowledge there is a problem but we want to do nothing about it. Third, we can admit a problem exists and vigorously search for a solution.

Most of us know when we're depressed because we've been there before. We recognize the symptoms. They don't vary a whole lot from one episode to another.

The mere nature of depression saps your willpower. It destroys the desire to fight. Your own thoughts war against you, telling you it's hopeless; you can't win. And yet, you eventually emerged from depression every time in the past. Some singles may be in a depressed state for years, but I suspect they did not consult a doctor or therapist. Treatment can be remarkably effective today. I want you to lose any prejudice you may have toward treatment and enlist it. You're literally in a fight for your life here.

Your goal when you are depressed is to take that third approach to a problem: I admit a problem exists (my depression), and I will vigorously search for an effective solution until I find one.

Hope in Christ's healing power

Your source of hope during depression is Christ's healing power. The gospels give us only an overview of Jesus' life. We know he did many healings, but the text does not go into great detail about what each healing was. It's safe to assume psychological illness existed then as well, including depression, and that Jesus healed it.

Christian denominations take a variety of views toward healing. Some hold healing services where there is a laying on of hands, others have somber prayer services, while many churches barely acknowledge God heals at all. Personally, I believe in medical science and doctors, but it's difficult to convince some pastors depression is as legitimate an illness as cancer. They might try to tell you it's "all in your head." Of course it is, but it may also be in your glands, your brain chemistry, your reproductive organs and several other places within your body.

Healing is a complicated business. God gave humanity intelligence and we have used it to relieve pain, break the grip of disease, and lengthen life. There's an old joke that "God does the healing but the doctor gets the money." I think it's always a combination of doctors and God. Doctors cannot heal without God, but God *can* heal without doctors.

In the case of depression, that's why I recommend going to a doctor. Depressed people don't think clearly. You may feel you've heard from God or may interpret something as a sign from God when it's only a case of unhealthy thinking. And, of course, if there's a physical cause to your depression, only a doctor is qualified to spot that. You might pray and pray and pray, waiting for God to answer you with healing, when one trip to a physician might put you on the path to feeling better within a week or two.

I have prayed for healing. In my long lifetime I have seen a handful of miraculous cures of other people, but it has never happened in my own life. Many Christians believe the dramatic manifestations of the spirit--prophecy, speaking in tongues, physical healing--were for the apostolic age and don't have a place in the modern church. Frankly, I don't know. But it's my impression so-called "faith healing" is more autosuggestion than it is genuine Holy Spirit healing.

When it comes to a faith healing or laying on of hands of someone who is depressed, the ill person is expected to proclaim an instant cure, which may be only an emotional reaction to the charged atmosphere of the service. Later, when they go home and depressed feelings return, they feel guilty and conclude the problem must be with them instead of with the minister. Confusion and more depression can follow.

We, as singles, can be sure Christ wants us to be healed of our depression. It's wise to learn from your suffering, but it's unwise to suffer when you don't have to. Don't let it drag on.

Depression is both an internal and external problem for single people. We can take steps to assist Christ's healing power or we can do nothing, waiting for him to do it all. Honestly, I try not to pray for miracle cures when I can take steps myself to get healing started. While each of us has experienced minor miracles that have no other explanation, I prefer to let God do that kind of dramatic healing for people who are teetering between life and death.

By the very nature of depression, you feel listless. You don't believe you can muster the strength to work your way out of the pit, and you'd be right. But with Jesus' healing power, you *can* work together with him to come back to normal. A healing doesn't have to be miraculous for God to be involved, although when you look back, it can sure seem as if it were. Perhaps the hardest move for a depressed person is finding the courage to reach up and take God's hand when he starts to lead you out. When everything seems hopeless, that's a scary thing to do.

Often in the gospels we find Jesus asking the ill person what they want him to do for them. In the case of blind or lame people, that seems like an unnecessary question, but at the root of it is Christ leading the person to focus their desire and belief that Jesus can actually help them. This first step of faith is the hardest. Again, we go back to the father of the sick boy in Mark 9:24:

"I do believe; help me overcome my unbelief!"

As depressed people needing Christ's healing, that's our cry too. We want to believe he can help us, but our own mental condition is fighting us. We need supernatural help with our faith. We need more than willpower to overcome our unbelief.

One of the toughest tasks when you are depressed is to not give up on God. Your faith may be at its lowest, but God is not gone. You can't feel him in your life, but as we have learned, emotions are not reliable, especially now. Feelings are not facts.

Reading positive Christian books can help. I have included a list of Books You'll Want to Read at the end of Hope for Hurting Singles. You may not be able to concentrate enough to read your Bible, but many Bibles have verses arranged by topic, such as verses to read when you're hurting or depressed or lonely. Track down that section in your Bible or look it up on the Internet. You might want to write the most meaningful verse on a note card to put in your pocket or purse. Work on committing it to memory. Remember, God's Word is truth. When you fill your mind with Scripture you are fortifying it against Satan's attacks and rebuilding your faith. Bible verses are *not* affirmations you're using to try to convince yourself of something. This is God's truth, the way things really are, and as it sinks into your subconscious, the Holy Spirit uses it in your healing.

When it comes to depression, your source of hope is Christ who saved you. You might have expected me to say that, but I mean it in a slightly different way. Many pastors say Jesus can meet all your needs. Let me rephrase that: Many married pastors say Jesus can meet all your needs. If he could, his Father would not have said, *"It is not good for the man to be alone."*

No, I mean Christ can help bring you out of your depression, keep you out of it, and give you the wisdom to see life clearly. Jesus is the supernatural helper you need to return to emotional stability, because you can't do it on your own. Even with professional help, you need God's healing power to restore your soul.

Seeing life clearly may bring sadness. It did for me. Jesus pulled me out of sadness, though, because he is the source of hope in all circumstances. When he was talking about how hard it is for rich people to be saved,

> *Jesus looked at them and said, "With man this is impossible, but not with God; all things are possible with God." (Mark 10:27)*

We need to be realistic about our hopes and dreams. Part of growing up is realizing some dreams don't come true, but on the other hand, many of us give up when marriage and other desires could still happen.

When Jesus said "all things are possible with God," he did mean all.

Chapter Five
Look in the Right Place for Self-Esteem

~~~~~
=====

Love your neighbor as yourself.
Jesus of Nazareth (Matthew 22:39)

Christians should have the highest self-esteem of anyone on earth, but surprisingly, that's often not the case.

As a people, we have been persecuted since the time of Jesus. Today the ridicule is as intense as ever. While we may not be fed to the lions or crucified in the arena, we are still the objects of mockery and insults, and our religion is scorned as naive superstition.

Many single Christians assume an extra burden by basing their self-esteem on their relationship status. If you are half of a couple, you feel confident and strong. If you are not currently in a relationship, you may feel lonely and depressed, less than a whole person. As usual, we let society dictate the standards while we struggle to achieve them.

Self-esteem is a facet of personality that involves thousands of contributing factors, from the way you were raised to personal accomplishments to how you feel about your physical appearance. Make no mistake about it, advertisers know our weaknesses better than we do, and they play to them to try to make us buy their products. Some ad agencies even hire psychologists so they can gear their pitches to potential customers' perceived shortcomings.

I wrote advertising for many years, took courses in advertising, and learned the tricks of the trade. My ads were very effective because I discovered how to push customers' "hot buttons." I knew their desires; I understood their attitudes. Even so, writing ads was not my full time career. Those men and women who devote their entire lifetime to it get paid huge salaries because they are so skilled at manipulating people's emotions. They can almost guarantee results.

What does that mean for you and me, as single Christians? Like our nonbeliever friends, we also have predictable desires. We want to be admired. We want others to see us as successful. Most of all, we want to feel good about ourselves.

Christians are caught in an odd trap. On one hand, we want to be respected by our peers, but on the other hand we are constantly told to guard against pride. We need to have a certain amount of pride in ourselves to function effectively in the world, yet if we cross over a line (and who knows where that is?), we fall into the sin of arrogance, which God hates. Sadly, many of us were so cowed in our youth that we can't even accept an honest compliment without feeling guilty.

There's definitely something wrong.

One of our goals, as single Christians, is to develop godly self-esteem. That may sound contradictory; however, our example is always Jesus himself. He was a person of supreme confidence. At the same time, he was the most humble person who ever walked the earth. He healed the blind and raised the dead while taking no credit for himself. He said, "Very truly I tell you, the Son can do nothing by himself;" (John 5:19, NIV)

Throughout this chapter we will consider the forces of the world that did not exist in Jesus' day, how we can counteract them and arrive at self-esteem that honors God. We have big things to do. If we want to serve God and live a meaningful life, we can't be wallflowers.

Judging from my email, many singles have low self-esteem because they believe they are incomplete without a spouse. "If no one has chosen me," they think, "then there must be something wrong with me." Singles with that mindset are especially vulnerable.

When you think about advertising, magazine and newspaper articles, television shows, and even the news, you find people setting a standard who don't always have your best interest at heart. I don't mean there's an evil conspiracy, but it is true that ads are meant to shape opinion and belief. By shaping your beliefs, they can sell things to you. One advertising course I took gave this simple guideline: "Convince the consumer they have a problem and that your product or service is the solution to it."

Start to study ads and commercials and you'll see this is true. From bad breath to dusty floors to getting lost in unfamiliar territory, these problems are thrust at us. The mouth wash, mops, and GPS devices are pushed as the solution. Don't get me wrong. Some of these things are legitimate problems and the products solve them well, saving us time and money.

The fine line comes in when commercials and ads try to persuade you there's something wrong with **you**. Sure, deodorant is a worthwhile solution to what's wrong with our armpits. But is there something wrong with us that a luxury car will fix? No. That's a subtle case of pitching to our sense of pride. If we have that fancy "whatever," then people will envy us and we'll feel better about ourselves.

Except that it doesn't work.

America is the most materialistic country on earth. People draw their self-esteem from what they own and display. Our entire economy is based on consumption, much of it unnecessary.

We want to be independent, but at the same time we want to follow the herd. Show off in the right way and you're idolized. Fail to conform with the group and you're knocked down. That's the problem in your life and mine. For most of us, the problem is self-esteem that is too **low**, not overinflated. We all like attention. The affirmation we receive from applause or a simple compliment helps us believe that we are, in fact, all right.

In 1985, actor Sally Field was viciously mocked simply because in her acceptance speech for the Academy Award for the film *Norma Rae*, she said, "You like me. You like me!" She merely expressed what most people feel. Did the many actors who have overdosed on drugs believe people **liked** them? Do people who go into alcohol rehab believe people **like** them? Aren't all of us a bit surprised when other people **like** us?

When it comes from the wrong place, our self-esteem can be as fragile as a tiny blown glass figurine. A single word, even a cross look can shatter it. When it comes from the right place, our self-esteem can endure criticism, failure, job loss, illness, divorce, and the whole spectrum of human tragedy.

If you looked closely at people striving to climb higher and higher, you could see the struggles they went through to get people to like them. And, they believe, if others like them, maybe they'll finally like themselves.

The answer is out there, and it doesn't lie in impressive possessions or stunning accomplishments. It lies, instead, in the same place Jesus looked: the love of his Father.

But you may be skeptical. Influenced by the relentless voices of advertising, you may be a product of this world.

You may be following the example of your parents or someone you admire. You may even have seen the world's ways work in the life of a friend, deciding that's the route for you too. Except in California, perhaps, self-esteem is not something we are taught in school. We watch people around us, we copy the ones we admire. We do things we think will get us praise. Some of us try to conform. Some of us try to rebel.

We get mixed messages from parents and teachers. In the classroom, we're given points for following the rules. Good behavior is even listed on our report card. But at the same time, we're taught about rebels like Patrick Henry, Harriet Tubman, and Martin Luther King Jr. and told we should be like them. How can you conform and rebel at the same time?

We want to feel good about ourselves, so we cut through the confusion by taking the paths successful people have taken. As Christians, we quickly realize the role models the world holds up are shams. Many have low morals. Many dally with drugs and alcohol, winking at the rule-makers because it's cool to disobey. Politicians and military leaders let us down with scandals.

We must be in this world but not of this world. Over and over we are warned in Scripture that the world's ways do not work. They do not bring the true happiness we seek. The call of the world is strong because Satan is the ruler of this world and his forces are relentless. We have become so sophisticated we ignore the truth that an invisible war is being waged.

Get off the performance treadmill

This performance treadmill turns countless people into workaholics, but it's about much more than earning extra money. Many of us desire to prove our worth through our accomplishments. We singles are especially prone to try to measure up with our deeds. As Christians we know we can't earn our salvation; that argument is settled. Still, we attempt to earn our self-esteem by working harder.

The world loves a hard worker. Even the Bible warns against laziness. I believe in having pride in my work and doing the best I'm capable of. We can rightfully feel good about ourselves when we give a task our best effort. The problem comes in when we try to earn love and respect. Ironically, our best effort is usually not good enough.

You may have had a demanding parent who was impossible to please. No matter what you did, you could never measure up. That deals a damaging blow to your self-esteem. All through life you fight to prove yourself, and just when you think you have, the company you thought you had impressed lays you off, or your romantic partner tells you they have found someone they like better.

The hard lesson to learn about performance is we must do it for *ourselves*, not for the approval of others.

Others may not appreciate your effort. They may deliberately ignore your performance just to spite you. Circumstances may come up where all your hard work just doesn't matter.

Many years ago I worked for a utility company in Peoria, Illinois as its publications director. I was in charge of writing and editing the monthly employee magazine. It was a tough job that required accuracy, creativity, and a desire to educate the 2,000 employees and retirees on issues important to them. After I had done nine monthly issues, management announced a company-wide layoff because of a reduction in force. The lowest seniority employees in all departments were cut, and I was low man in the Communications Department.

When the vice president of our division told me I was being dismissed, he said, "Our company magazine has never looked better since you took it over, but I'm afraid we have to let you go."

They didn't try to make a place for me because I was a hard worker. They didn't give me a break because I surpassed the goals set for me and more. They didn't even promise to hire me back when times got better.

Did my self-esteem take a hit? You better believe it! When the rumors of the layoffs started, one of my coworkers in the Communications Department was anxious he might get laid off. He acted as company spokesman to the news media, had many years of service, and was respected by everyone.

I told him, "Tom, you don't have anything to worry about."

But Tom had been laid off before, from another company. So had Neil, another nervous communications employee. They both told me, "Once you've been laid off, you're never the same."

They were right. After that, I vowed to keep working as hard as ever and doing the best job I could, but only for my personal pride in my work. I had learned the hard lesson that building your self-esteem on achievements is building on a foundation of sand. It can crumble at any time.

Too many of us singles pour our heart and soul into our career because we get affirmation from it. A compliment from the boss makes you feel good. A raise in pay or promotion makes you think the company appreciates your hard work. But as much as your workplace might feel like a "family," don't be fooled. It's fine to be friends with your coworkers, but keep in mind your job is always a business contract. It can end at any time.

Important positions with high pay can impress your parents or family. You may buy them expensive presents at

Christmas. They're proud of you and brag to their friends about how well you're doing. Better they should be proud of your **character** and the kind of person you are.

Your character is something you can control.
Your "success" is not.

How many movie stars have you seen who were on every magazine cover and were the hottest thing going--until they weren't? The public is fickle. It's always looking for something new. One minute celebrities are making millions, and a few years later they're in rehab because their time has come and gone. Unable to see through the idol worship, they fail to plan ahead so they can retire gracefully.

I don't want to give you the wrong impression. I believe we should all give our employer our best effort. When I was working, I made it a game with myself to try to outdo my previous month's work or my previous year's accomplishments. I worked hard to achieve the goals my boss set for me. We all owe our employer our best for the pay we receive. Extra effort can often earn a promotion and more pay. More pay is a good thing.

I never advocate goofing off because you don't like your pay or working conditions. I don't want to imply that you become cynical and give anything less than your best effort because you may get laid off. You have an obligation to your employer and to God to be conscientious in your career.

My point, however, is that you can't build your self-esteem on your career. Eventually you'll retire, as I did. It's a tough adjustment. Men, especially, feel working is a key part of their masculinity. In fact, a former coworker retired from the place we both worked, then immediately got another job. When I saw him in a store and he told me about it, I said, "Bob, you've earned a rest."

He replied, deadly serious, "I believe a man isn't a man unless he's working."

Eventually Bob will reach a point physically when he **won't** be able to work. Then what will he be?

No, your self-esteem has to be based on something that cannot change, and the only thing safe from change is the love God has for you.

Performance is a treadmill that keeps you running until you're exhausted, and when you finally shut it down, you find you've gotten nowhere. You're exhausted. You scratch your head and ask, "Now what do I do?"

The love of God, on the other hand, is constant whether you're a high achiever or struggling to make ends meet. God doesn't care how much money you make or what kind of car you drive. It doesn't matter to him how many degrees you have behind your name or whether you have none at all. He doesn't care whether you wear designer clothes or things from the resale shop. Your grandiose achievements don't impress him one bit.

God, the most important being in the Universe, loves you simply because you're you. *"I the Lord do not change,"* God tells us in Malachi 3:6. Because **he** doesn't change, his love for you doesn't change, either. He's not like a fickle public who loves you when you're up and forgets you when you're down.

This world, on the other hand, is changing constantly and faster than ever. Even your life can change in an instant. A stroke or other debilitating illness can end your high-performance career tomorrow. Everybody who was so impressed with you may neglect you, but God never will. He is even closer to you in hard times than in good times.

Be a good employee. Do the best you can. Make your company successful and fulfill your obligation to them, but keep things in perspective. Understand that performance is something you do, not who you are. The first thing a new acquaintance asks you is "What do you do?", but that's not where your self-esteem comes from. That's what you're doing **now**. It's not necessarily what you'll be doing ten years from now.

A million years from now, when your career seems like a faded moment in eternity, you will still be loved by Almighty God. That should make you feel so good you want to dance with joy. He has chosen you to love. He has chosen you to save, and he's so enthralled with you that he wants you to be with him for time without end. I don't know about you, but it gives me goosebumps!

Getting off the performance treadmill will change your life. Knowing you don't have to measure up to receive God's love is the most liberating experience on earth. Accepting that you were created for the sole purpose of him loving you is the most powerful self-esteem truth any of us can possess. Keep it in your heart. Think of it every day. That's where your real worth lies.

Why you can't please everyone

One of the disappointing truths you learn in grade school is that everybody isn't going to like you. Unfortunately, some poor souls never learn that lesson and go through life believing they can please everyone. When they find they can't, they blame themselves rather than the other person and wonder what is wrong. They never consider that the other person may have the problem.

Jesus commanded us to love one another, but even Christians can't do that without his help. We're not immune to jealously or prejudice. Some people are hard to love. They're cruel and thoughtless and care only about themselves. It's understandable why they don't have a long line of fans. But you and I, who try to be decent human beings, are sometimes baffled why others seem to have it in for us.

People who have not received a lot of love find it hard to love others. Maybe they don't know how. Maybe they're doing it out of self-protection: They figure they can't get hurt if they don't make themselves vulnerable. Then there are others, and you may find this hard to believe, who are envious of you. You may not think you have any qualities other people could envy, but you'd be surprised. They withhold their approval to try to get back at you.

The games don't stop when we graduate from high school. To grow and become a better person, you have to be willing to admit your mistakes and eliminate bad behavior. Many people have such low self-esteem they can't do that. They keep doing the same childish things all their life. If you haven't encountered anyone like that yet, trust me, you will.

Much of it hinges on forgiveness. If I am able to forgive myself for my faults, I am better able to forgive my neighbor for theirs. But if that person is unable to even **admit** they have faults, let alone forgive himself or herself, they're certainly not going to forgive you.

It's exhausting trying to please everyone. You can't do it. If Jesus, the only perfect person who ever lived, was unable to please everyone, why should you and I think we can? When you understand that some people aren't going to like you no matter what, it actually does something positive for your self-esteem. It takes the pressure off. You don't have to stay awake at night worrying why Lynn or Jeff doesn't like you despite your best efforts. You can treat them decently and be polite but put them in the category of people whose approval you'll probably never get. Yes, you are to love them, but it's not your fault if they don't return your love.

If you follow Jesus Christ and you're serious about it, people are going to reject you, even if you don't wear a cross on a chain around your neck proclaiming you're a Christian. *"Blessed are you when people hate you, when they exclude you and insult you and reject your name as evil, because of the Son of Man,"* Jesus said. (Luke 6:22) There's something about you they don't like. Your attitude is different. You don't exactly fit in. They resent your confidence. They don't understand your joy.

For many years I didn't get this. I couldn't figure out why other people didn't like me. Of course I considered the probability that I had some obnoxious habits or had done something to offend them, but I saw that in many instances I was not the only person they didn't like. They had hate for a lot of people.

I had a boss I could not please. No matter what I did, she found a way to pick it apart. She gave me demeaning lectures on the tiniest of mistakes. She was the only person to ever call me "incompetent." Then I learned she did the same thing to the two other editors in our office. I also learned there was a revolving door turnover in her department because no one could please her. I realized the deck was stacked against me and I didn't want to live that way. I found another job, with better pay, and my new boss treated me like I was a godsend! I hadn't changed. What **did** change was I got a new boss who understood absolute perfection in our fast-paced, demanding line of work was counterproductive. He encouraged his subordinates when we did a good job and was compassionate in his criticism.

Whether it's your employer, a girlfriend or boyfriend, your parents, or someone else in your life, you can only do your best, but you can't let your self-esteem rest on their approval. As Robert S. McGee says in his book, *The Search for Significance*:

We do not have to be successful or have to be pleasing to others to have a healthy sense of self-esteem and worth. That worth has freely and conclusively been given to us by God. Failure and/or the disapproval of others can't take it away! Therefore, we can conclude, It would be nice to be approved by my parents (or whomever), but if they don't approve of me, I'm still loved and accepted by God. (p. 29-30)

It may take you years to grasp and accept this truth, but once you do, you will finally have an accurate picture of your worth. When you base your self-esteem on the love and acceptance of God, you can see why trying to please everyone is an impossible task. Paradoxically, the one with the highest standards already approves you. You are pleasing to God because of what Christ has done for you. God has adopted you as one of his children. He is motivated by love and love alone. When your self-esteem depends on him, it's in good hands.

Rewrite your self-esteem story

Reading this and putting it into action in your life are two different things. You may agree with everything I've said about self-esteem but still struggle to apply it. Our feelings of worthlessness run deep. They've been reinforced by years of repetition. Changing them will be hard.

Even so, the Holy Spirit stands ready to help. He is also called the Spirit of Truth because one of his roles is to reveal the truth to you and make it real in your life. As you allow yourself to be open to his teaching, he unfolds Scripture so it takes on new meaning. The Bible is a unique book in that it speaks a specific, individualized message to each person reading it. It is God's instruction book to you, personally.

More than anything else, the Bible is the greatest source of hope in your life. In no uncertain terms, it spells out God's love for you. Every book in it points to Christ, and Christ died for you. It's well worth your time to use a concordance or online tool to look up Bible verses that affirm God's love for you, write them on 3" x 5" index cards, and commit them to memory. Then, when one of these self-esteem-rattling situations arises, you can quickly bring the truth to mind to counteract your emotional reaction.

As you rewrite your self-esteem story, you can't erase all the painful episodes from your past, but with God's help, you **can** see them differently. You can understand the negative effect they had on your life. You can begin to know why you think about yourself the way you do. Best of all, you can use God's acceptance of you to dismiss your self-critical thoughts. Who are you to argue with God? If he says you're lovable, he knows best! All of us argue with God at times, but haven't you found out he always wins? That's because he's running things and we're not, and give thanks for that!

Your past can't be changed, but it *can* be reinterpreted.

We're almost always too hard on ourselves. We singles have a lot of time to think, and too often we use it to beat ourselves up. That's tough on your self-esteem and you need to stop it. Remember, you did the best you could at the time, with the information you had. In retrospect, you can see where you might have done or said something differently, but the good news is the Holy Spirit can help you forgive yourself for past mistakes. And you already know God forgives your sins every time you ask him.

The Holy Spirit can also help you understand other people's motives. When a painful situation was happening, you were too emotionally involved to see things accurately, but with the passage of time and God's help, you can get a clearer perspective. We each pursue our own needs. People who tried to control you in the past thought they were doing you a favor by criticizing you or trying to make you do things their way. That doesn't make them right, of course, but it does help you see the why behind what happened.

Growth takes time. The stronger something is, the more time it takes. A willow tree grows quickly, but its wood is soft and weak. An oak tree grows very slowly, but its wood is hard and strong. You want "oak tree self-esteem." You want a sense of worth that stands up to the knocks and stresses of life.

As you're rewriting your self-esteem story, you'll have setbacks. Events will happen that will drive you into depression. Some people will still be able to hurt you with their cutting remarks. Be patient with yourself. Smash that destructive self-talk with your Bible verses about God's love. Ask yourself why certain people get under your skin. Ask the Holy Spirit to reveal to you why they do it. Calmly plan how you're going to respond the next time they try it.

And pray. Building healthy self-esteem is a lifelong project. Something this important requires a lot of conversation with God. It shouldn't be formal, like prayers you recite in church. Don't use "thee's" and "thou's." Talk to him the way you talk to your best friend, because that's what he is. You'll feel more comfortable and be more natural. Prayer is your secret weapon when you're trying to make a major change in your life.

With God as your ally, you will find over time that fewer things bother you. You'll be able to shrug off remarks that in the past would have brought tears. You'll be able to separate constructive criticism from mean-spirited insults. You'll ask God for strength and wisdom and receive it.

Eventually you'll develop a spirit of boldness. Instead of questioning your importance, you'll trust God's evaluation of you rather than your own. Find hope in being able to say, as Paul did, *"If God is for us, who can be against us?"* (Romans 8:31)

Chapter Six
Take Back Your Life from Fear

≈≈≈≈≈

The only known antidote to fear is faith.
Woodrow Kroll

Let's talk about how you can have hope even when you're afraid.

When I was a young man, I read every self-help book I could get my hands on. Many were worthwhile but some were trash, written only to make a quick buck. Two of the classics are *How to Stop Worrying and Start Living*, by Dale Carnegie, and *The Power of Positive Thinking,* by Norman Vincent Peale. From those two books I learned the important truth that everyone is afraid.

Both authors interviewed important, powerful business executives. Those successful adults, whose names were disguised, confessed their fears of what you and I might consider trivial things. I read about their phobias with fascination, never suspecting that leaders of business and industry felt the same way I did. It helps to know that being afraid is normal and nothing to be ashamed of.

Many people deny their fears, others disguise them convincingly, but every person on earth has things they are afraid of. We singles fear many things, some with good reason and some not. The wise fears help us keep safe. They make us buckle our seatbelt, go to the doctor for regular checkups, and take out insurance.

But because we spend so much time alone, we singles tend to focus on our fears to the point of obsession. They color our thinking, preventing us from doing many of the things that would make for a happier life. We all rationalize. I've been guilty of saying, "That's just the way I am," even though I know that's the lamest excuse on earth. We're all capable of change, even in areas where we think we have a free pass because that's the way God made us.

Psychologists have dozens of theories on how to beat fear, and we'll discuss some of those in this chapter. Many Christians discount the value of psychology and therapy, but I think they're helpful. I've never gone overboard trying to psychoanalyze myself and I've never been in therapy. However, knowing about psychology does help you understand why you do certain things.

When it comes to psychology, no one was more skilled in that area than Jesus Christ. We usually don't think of him in that way because the Bible never uses the word "psychology." In its rather archaic way, it talks of a what's in a person's heart. Today we know the heart is nothing more than a sophisticated muscle. A person's feelings and motives are in their mind.

Jesus understood the human mind so well because he helped create it. One of his most frequent commands in the gospels was "Don't be afraid," or "Fear not." He knew the immense power of fear. Today, if I told someone in crisis "Don't be afraid," I would be considered shallow. The difference between Jesus saying that and me saying that is Jesus knows things I don't. He sees behind the veil, so to speak. He knows the future and can speak with assurance. Through the Bible, Jesus still speaks to you across the centuries. He tells you "Don't be afraid," and he can say that sincerely because he knows things are going to turn out for good for you in the end.

Singles' two greatest fears

Judging from the emails I get from my web site, *www.inspiration-for-singles.com,* singles' greatest fears are never marrying and growing old alone. I can't belittle those fears because I've had them myself. They are real and legitimate. I'm not going to say, "Oh, you have nothing to worry about. You'll get married and live happily ever after."

Maybe you won't get married. I have never been married. I can't say I will live the rest of my life this way. Maybe I will get married at some point. I honestly don't know, but I can tell you this much truthfully: I'm not afraid of being alone any more.

Somewhere along the way, I surrendered my future to Christ. I stopped demanding he help me find a wife and get married. That's not a cop-out. I didn't give up and throw in the towel, but I put my destiny in God's hands, promising to live with whatever he decides for me.

If you want to be married, whether you're 21 or 71, I suggest a proactive approach. If I have any regrets in life, it's that I wasn't more assertive in every area. Good things come to people who zealously go after them. That's worth remembering. I often say God is not going to drop a Prince (or Princess) Charming in your lap. It takes more than praying. It takes action.

Action is the element that overcomes fear. Tough men, soldiers and pilots who have been under fire in war, all say the same thing about fear: Everybody with any sense is afraid in combat. Courage, they say, is not the absence of fear but going ahead and doing what you must in spite of fear.

That's the key to getting what you want in life, whether it's a good marriage or a successful career. You can't let fear stop you. You have to be bigger than your fear, pushing ahead no matter what. Whenever I have had to do something I feared, I did it not through human willpower but through knowing Christ stands with me. The Christian life is about receiving strength from God. We can't do it on our own.

So if you want to be married, are you doing everything you can to increase your opportunities? It will require going outside your comfort zone. You'll have to forge ahead regardless. Again, God always stands ready to help you with any worthwhile endeavor. The formula is simple: You have to meet the right person. What are you doing to meet him or her? Well, you can probably supply the methods, but you also have to impose standards. You want quality over quantity. You're going to find quantity in bars, but probably not quality. In our culture, players who hang out in bars are usually looking for only one thing, and it's not marriage.

In the chapter on shyness, you learned several strategies to beat that common obstacle. How great would it be if there were a club for shy singles? The only problem is attendance at meetings would probably be dismal. Since there isn't such a club, you have to change from being a shy person to being a bold person. That's where God's help comes in.

First you must believe you can change. Overcoming fear is a matter of maturity. Maturity is not, as our society tries to convince us, old age. Maturity is making wise decisions, and even young people can do that. You can do that. If you go to a bar in search of a mate, maturity will tell you the consequences will probably be bad. If you take a class or go out with someone recommended by a friend or relative, maturity tells you the odds are better of a good outcome with this approach. In the chapter on rejection, we dealt with how to handle disappointing events. The important thing to remember is that action produces opportunities. More action produces more opportunities. Just like panning for gold, the more you do it, the better your chances of finding a nugget!

Today, Internet dating provides opportunities that didn't exist when I was young. However, I have learned from several single women that even Christian dating sites are packed with predators trying to bed vulnerable young women. These men have no shame about lying on their profile. What seems like a perfect match can turn out to be a nightmare, and that's what frightens women off. As disgusting as that is, it happens in offline dating as well. You know the necessary precautions for dating today. It's sad, but that's part of the process.

The only way we can conquer our fears in such a situation is to take all the wise precautions, go ahead, and proceed very slowly. It's smart to be alert to danger signs all along the way. With a vigilant attitude, you can see whether the other person is trustworthy. Danger signs include lying, requests for money, concocted excuses, drinking too much, and aggressiveness. Don't make the mistake of thinking you can "reform" the other person. It doesn't work and will only end in heartache. Too many women get stuck with deadbeat men because they thought they could improve their behavior with "a little work."

Respect yourself. Don't give in to the temptation to take abuse, with the inevitable apologies and excuses afterward. Abusers, whether physical or emotional, are the lowest form of manipulators. Run far and fast and don't give them a second chance!

Let me tell you there are many quality Christian singles available simply because they tend not to be aggressive. Most often Christian men are shy and may have been hurt in an earlier relationship. Yes, men **do** have feelings and we **do** get hurt.

Worthwhile things are seldom easy. If you want to find a good, loving spouse, you'll have to work through your fears, with God's help, and put up with some unpleasantness. If you lower your standards just to be married, it will come back to haunt you. Writer Josh McDowell said being alone is not the worst thing in life. The worst thing is being with the wrong person.

Fear of running out of money

Most of us spend too much because we've never been taught to save. We also get used to luxuries we mistake for necessities. Millions of singles, especially in their 40s and 50s, are afraid of ending up broke. It's a legitimate fear, and again, it should move you to take action.

It seems as if the economy is **always** bad, the job market is **always** tight, and things are **always** too expensive. Then there's the common experience among singles I call "gift lift." That's buying yourself a gift because you've had a bad day or you've been told to reward yourself. My brother Dave calls it "anesthesia." We do it trying to ease the pain of everyday living, but it never works. Listen to what Jesus said about it 2,000 years ago:

> *"Watch out! Be on your guard against all kinds of greed; life does not consist in an abundance of possessions." (Luke 12:15)*

For most of us, being financially secure requires sacrifice, and that's the last thing singles want to do. When you're plagued by loneliness, denying yourself nice things seems too much to bear. That explains most credit card debt. People are ashamed or unable to say, "I can't afford it." When you learn to say "no," you start on the path to solvency.

I have always been a saver. I learned long ago that some kind of crisis always comes up. After I had an emergency appendectomy and cancer within six months, I had $13,000 in medical bills, despite the fact that I had health insurance. It was an indescribable feeling to be able to pay those bills off from my savings. One of the advantages of being single is you can be a tightwad and nobody complains! When you don't have a spouse and children, you can save money by cutting back here and there.

Singles who are barely getting by may think it's impossible for them to put money aside for an emergency. No matter how little money I made during my career, I made it a point to save **something**, if only a couple dollars a week. It grows over time. It's a hard choice to deny yourself things, made even worse if your friends are teasing you about being cheap. But when that emergency comes up--and one always does--it's an oh-so-sweet feeling to be able to pay for it.

In my ebook *How to Master Your Money*, I suggest singles get a professional financial adviser as early in life as possible. The common misconception is that financial advisers are only for the rich. That's not true. A skilled financial adviser can help **make** you rich.

Investing wisely is the right action to take against the fear of running out of money. That's not greed. It's using what God gave you to provide for your future, exactly what Joseph did in the book of Genesis to protect the Egyptians against the coming famine. You'll recall that he stored away the surplus grain in the good years. When the lean years hit, as Pharaoh's dream predicted, Joseph was ready. What could have been deadly was prevented because Joseph saved.

With the upheaval in world stock markets in the past several years, many singles have to work longer than expected to retire, which makes saving and investing more important than ever. We all need to resist the messages blasted at us. Stores encourage you to buy, buy, buy. If you can't afford to pay for it, they want you to put it on your credit card. Keep in mind that all this "easy financing" is in the store's best interest, not yours. Clerks may treat you courteously when you're ringing up the debt, but believe me, the credit card company or collection agency won't be nearly as polite when the payments come due.

Being able to provide for your future requires learning to ruthlessly say "no." At the big box discount store in my city, every time I check out, the clerk asks me if I want to apply for their store credit card. It might be easier to do it so I could answer, "I already have one," but I truly don't need more than one credit card. Having multiple cards just makes it that much easier to max out several and pile up more debt. Make no mistake: Anything a store pushes that aggressively is in **their** favor, not yours.

Whether it's denying yourself the latest fashion, shopping at a you-bag-it grocery store or driving an older car (mine is currently 18 years old and I expect to get several more years out of it), when it comes to money, you owe it to yourself to save for your retirement now to avoid fear of running out of money later.

This runs contrary to our spend, spend, spend culture, but I can guarantee you'll be happy you made the sacrifice. We singles can't count on an inheritance. We can't count on the government to provide for us. We certainly can't count on winning the Lottery. But we can count on our own foresight and planning to provide for our future.

Please get this into your head in no uncertain terms:

Saving for my retirement is *my* responsibility. Nobody else is going to do it for me. It's up to me to do it or it won't get done.

Healthy fear for your personal safety

Many singles, especially women, live in fear for their personal safety. Again, this is one of those "good" fears that leads you to watch out for yourself, but taken to extremes, it can smother your life and limit your opportunities.

I live in a small town of fewer than 20,000 people. The crime rate is fairly low. Muggings and robberies in my city are rare, but part of that is due to people here taking precautions. Also, it's harder to get away with crime in a small town. A criminal can't simply blend into the crowd and use the anonymity of the big city. While everyone doesn't know one another here, people **do** look out for their neighbors.

The world has changed. It's naive and dangerous to trust everyone. If you grew up in a large city, you have probably learned how to protect yourself, but if you are afraid, you can find a class on self-defense and personal safety through the YMCA, a college, or the local police department. If this fear is an problem for you, consider taking such a class. It can build your confidence and keep you safer.

Once we have taken all the precautions humanly possible, we have to turn this area over to God. The Bible gives us a good example of surrendering our safety to God. Listen to what David asked:

> *Keep me safe, LORD, from the hands of the wicked; protect me from the violent, who devise ways to trip my feet. (Psalm 140:4)*

For more than ten years, David's life was threatened by King Saul. David had done nothing wrong and had been chosen by God to be Israel's king, but Saul was jealous of him. David and his men fled through the hills. He knew real danger, the threat of execution. He did everything he could to avoid his pursuers, but at some point he had to turn it over to God.

As I mentioned earlier, I don't believe in taking unnecessary risks. As Christians, our bodies do not belong to us. The terrible price paid for our salvation was the crucifixion of Jesus Christ. In exchange for our salvation, we now belong to him. But I also believe God pledges his protection. Our lives are in his hands. Christians are killed at young ages by traffic accidents, disease, and war, but we can rest assured they go quickly into the arms of God. God alone knows the length of our days. We have no right to shorten them, but on the other hand, he will protect us until our work on earth is finished. To believe that is to trust our heavenly Father for our safety.

Living in constant fear is a debilitating experience. I know. If you sincerely trust in God, you must turn your fears over to him, including fear for your personal safety. Only then can you experience the freedom Christ's death bought for you.

Why we fear illness

One of the real fears of being single is getting sick, with no one to take care of you. But many singles go beyond that. They are afraid of becoming seriously ill and become obsessed about it. Our modern media doesn't help. Watch television for an hour and you're bombarded with pharmaceutical commercials promising cures for ailments you've never even heard of. Every week there's a news story about the dangers of eating red meat or drinking soda or not getting enough exercise. A sensitive person who paid attention to all those warnings could quickly become paranoid that they either had some deadly disease or were soon about to get one.

Aches and pains are like things that go bump in the night. When you're living alone, they get magnified. Soon the psychosomatic effect takes over and what started out as indigestion escalates into heartburn or something worse. A slight twinge becomes a roaring headache.

I'm not making fun of singles who do this. I used to be one. I understand too well how we can worry about our health, making the situation worse than it is. An overactive imagination is one of the real dangers of the single life. Not all singles are excessively concerned with their health, so if it isn't a problem for you now, please keep reading so it doesn't become one in the future.

I don't want to burden you with my medical history except to tell you that I've had cancer twice, the first time when I was 25 years old. In the year or two after my treatments, every ache and pain terrified me. I was afraid my cancer had come back or that a new one had started. I was living in terror. I was miserable.

Finally, after a couple false alarms at the doctor's office, I decided I didn't want to live that way the rest of my life. I resolved to go for regular checkups and watch for the warning signs, but I wasn't going to spoil my happiness with fear of getting cancer again. That wasn't an easy thing to do. I was often tempted by minor twinges, but once I was able to calm myself, they went away.

We each have to reach a happy, sensible medium. We can't ignore our health, but we can't become consumed by it either. If you come from a family of hypochondriacs or where someone died at an early age, such a fear may be ingrained and hard to overcome. But worry is corrosive. It can actually **cause** health problems that wouldn't otherwise exist.

I can't tell you that winning over my health fears was an overnight victory. It wasn't. It took many years of reminding myself that I had been monitoring my health through regular physicals and if anything was wrong, they would have found it.

I also had to surrender my health to God.

As I've already said, surrendering your life to God is the toughest thing a Christian can do. Over and over in the Bible we see God urging us to trust in him. Real courage isn't found in bungee jumping, extreme sports, or risking your neck. It's found in having faith in God when everything inside shouts for you not to. And believe me, Satan will be adding his sly whispers to those shouts as well. When you trust God instead of yourself, Satan is dealt a real blow. Since God knows the future and never gives bad advice, you can stay out of trouble when you put your faith in him.

So what happened with me, then? Why did I get cancer a second time? Did God let me down? Did he fail me when I put my life in his hands?

That's not the way I see it. My first cancer and second cancer were were unrelated and 34 years apart. It's important for you to know that all four of my grandparents had cancer, three dying from it. My father died from cancer. My mother has also had cancer twice. With genetics like that, the odds were increased that I would get it.

As I grow older, I spend less and less time second-guessing God. I can't explain why my family is cancer prone or why I've had it twice any more than I can explain why some people are born blind or paralyzed or developmentally disabled. These are deep questions we'll only get the answer to on the other side.

With this kind of family history, I **do** know fear about cancer could easily dominate my life. I counter it by trusting in God, and that's what you have to do too. Whether it's heart problems, mental illness, stroke, debilitating diseases or some other hereditary issue, the best we can do is take prudent preventive measures and get on with our life. It's wise to be aware of the problems that plague us as singles so we can act to cancel them out. Fear of illness may strike you early on or it may not appear in your life until you're past 50 or 60.

God did not create you to live in a spirit of fear. Like other problems, fear puts a heavy weight in your backpack. Every night you go to bed exhausted. You don't sleep well. You wake up tired the next day then pick up that heavy backpack again. Take the weight of fear out of it. Hand it over to God. Let him carry it. You'll be able to do more, enjoy life more, and live up to your potential if you travel light.

Anxiety: The nameless fear

I sometimes find myself nervous and upset for no reason. Fear without a cause is anxiety. We live in an anxious culture. Take constant noise, stress, a breakneck pace, a bad diet and lack of sleep and you have a surefire formula for anxiety.

It's funny that we think of anxiety as a modern problem caused by our pressure-cooker world. Before there were cell phones, cars, planes, or computers, Jesus warned his followers about anxiety:

> Therefore do not be anxious, saying, 'What shall we eat?' or 'What shall we drink?' or 'What shall we wear?' (Matthew 6:31, ESV)

Right after that he gives the answer to anxiety:

But seek first the kingdom of God and his righteousness, and all these things will be added to you. (Matthew 6:33, ESV)

When it comes right down to it, our basic needs have not changed from Jesus' day: food, clothing and shelter. We may not be able to identify our anxiety in one of those neat categories, but Jesus' basic point was to focus on the kingdom of God first, confident God would take care of our needs--not wants--after that.

In the first century A.D., advertising did not exist. People in ancient Israel were not bombarded throughout their day with messages to buy this, do that, think this way. Most of the population was poor. They had no trouble telling the difference between needs and wants. Today, our anxieties come from dozens of different sources, producing a state of uneasiness in us. We'll cover this more fully in the chapter on peace of mind, but it's safe to say many singles are unsettled because they think they're not living up to someone's expectations for them, even though they don't know who they're supposed to please or what their expectations are!

This general state of jumpiness fits into the plans of advertisers, politicians, and government. They want you to try to restore your peace of mind by doing what they suggest. What a joke! They'll only leave you alone until they want your money, vote, or loyalty again.

Seek the kingdom of God, on the other hand, and you have a worthwhile focus. You have a target you can not only hit, but which has everlasting value. Christ and his ways are the great stabilizer in life, the anxiety-nullifier, if you will.

Of all the voices you hear, only one tells the truth, that of Jesus. He is concerned about **you**, not what he can get out of you. He is motivated by love, not selfish manipulation. When you allow the Holy Spirit to be your guide, you receive the ultimate in wisdom. Seek the kingdom of God first and you travel the path to heaven. Long after merchandise fads have gone and politics has vanished into the mists of the past, the kingdom of God is still the right way. Anxiety is unfocused fear. Seeking the kingdom of God is focused faith.

By reading the Bible, you can know what Jesus wants from you. By listening to the world, all you'll hear is a jumble of confusion. The world changes by the minute. God, on the other hand, never changes. Giving in to anxiety leads to a sense of agitation. Seeking the kingdom of God leads to peace.

Seeking the kingdom of God also gives you something to do, and that's important. While you can't earn your salvation, you can build your personal intimacy with Jesus Christ. Doing that gives you a worthy place to direct your energy. Instead of wasting your stamina with nervous fretting, you put it toward an end that will do you some good. More importantly, you can't seek the kingdom of God without increasing that kingdom for him.

The single life can be a garden for anxiety if we're not careful. Without a spouse to talk with in the evening to keep us balanced, we can give in to our imaginings, even when we're not able to articulate them to ourselves. Jesus' solution tells us what our duty is: Seek the kingdom of God first. In this world, that's a big enough chore to keep us busy 24/7.

If you do put God's kingdom first, as Jesus commands, it puts the rest of life in perspective, and that's something we singles badly need. It helps you make right decisions, stay out of trouble, and prepare for your future. It prevents you from wasting your life by running down the rabbit holes of success or fame. It keeps your attitude right toward money. Most of all, it reminds you that your relationship with God is your Number One Priority.

Reading the Bible should become natural to you whenever anxiety strikes. I don't expect you to sit at home every evening reading your Bible from after dinner to bed time, but the Bible is the place to go in times of trial. Reflecting on how Bible characters handled their situation, rightly or wrongly, gives you direction as to what you should do. Just filling your mind with the assurance of God's love for you trumps giving in to anxiety.

You can live in day-tight compartments. You can plan for your future but not obsess over the unknown. You can spend your thought-life seeking the Highest Good rather than worrying over a thousand "what if's?" These are concrete ways you can triumph over anxiety. When you have the **known** of the Holy Spirit, the **known** of your salvation, and the **known** of God's love, you don't have to squander your life being upset over life's unknowns.

How to do the impossible

Fear is a natural human emotion that affects every person on earth. Trying **not** to fear seems like doing the impossible, yet that's exactly what Jesus told his followers to do. We single followers, facing life without a helpmate (at least for the present!), seem to be at a disadvantage. But things are not always what they seem:

> *Jesus replied, "What is impossible with man is possible with God." (Luke 18:27)*

Our God is the great Worker Behind the Scenes. In the invisible world where God lives, his incomprehensible power affects the circumstances of the visible world. All miracles are not obvious. Only when you get to heaven will you see how God accomplished his plan in your life. Only then will you comprehend how he made the impossible possible.

In the meantime, you have to let go of your demand to understand everything about your life and simply put your trust in him. That's the only way you can overcome fear. Even that may sound like an impossible task if you have tried it in the past and failed.

It has been my experience that I possess very little power. I have tried to change circumstances so many times without success that I am bitterly reminded just how weak I am. In contrast, I see the majesty of the earth and stars and know my God created all of it just by speaking it into being. **That's** power, power to do the impossible.

Therefore, I believe this same God can help me beat my fear. I don't do that out of blind trust, but in a sort of logic that acknowledges Jesus knows things I don't know. He has the right to say, "Fear not," because he knows there is nothing to fear. I don't know that. When it comes to my fear, I operate on my feelings, not my knowledge. Angels told men "fear not" also. They too see behind the veil into the other world.

Most of us base our judgment on what we can see. God sees everything, not just this visible world. That makes all the difference. What's more, God holds the real power to change things.

Sometimes we can truly not fear; other times we have to push on despite fear. The latter calls for us to trust God no matter what happens. The martyrs trusted God but were not rescued. They died. Today they hold high respect in heaven.

This life is not all there is.

My goal in life is not to be a martyr but to trust God with my whole heart, as they did. If you and I can do that, we can see the impossible happen in our lives.

When you are afraid, and that is more common among singles and more frequent than you admit to others, your hope is in God. In this book about hope, we will return, time and again, to placing our focus on God and off ourselves. In the great miracles of the Bible, from the parting of the Red Sea to the raising of the dead, the deed was always done by God, with the cooperation of human beings. There is no miracle worker in the Bible except God, and that is still true today.

"The Christian life is a life that consists of following Jesus," said evangelist and Bible scholar A.W. Pink. That's a simple statement that contains a profound responsibility. If we singles are serious about following Jesus, we can't do it in one area of our life and not another. We can't go to church but avoid Jesus' teachings. We can't profess to be a Christian but choose our own way over Christ's. Following Jesus requires trust, particularly in the area of fear. If we don't trust God, we aren't following Jesus.

I have made a lot of mistakes in my life, but I try not to make the same mistake twice. I confess I repeatedly made the same mistake of not trusting God because my own fear got in the way. Coupled to whatever I was afraid of was my fear that God would not come through for me. As I grew older, I came to understand that my definition of "coming through" and God's definition of "coming through" were often exact opposites. It wasn't really a matter of God coming through. It was a matter of me getting my own way. When God's way didn't coincide with mine, it wasn't always pleasant. Relationships fell apart, I lost jobs, I lost writing opportunities I deeply wanted. It takes genuine humility to admit God is always right.

I'm not at that point yet.

I usually want my own way because I'm still under the illusion that sometimes I know better than God or that people will admire me more or that I'll be better off. I'm too thick to get that those things are not the point. The point is this: God wants to make me more like his Son, Jesus Christ.

Something I am learning is that God wants me to lose my fears because that will make me more like Jesus. The only time we see Jesus afraid is in the Garden of Gethsemane before his death, and his human nature had good reason to be afraid. But by the time he prayed and left the garden, he had accepted his Father's will for him and carried out his mission with boldness. How could he do that?

He trusted God.

Trusting God is good for you and me because it makes us more like Christ. Handing our fears over to our Father is the wisest thing to do. Everything in our selfish human nature argues against it, but the Christian life can't be lived solely through our human nature. We must have the help of the Holy Spirit. We are sure to fail without it.

The takeaway I want you to remember from this chapter about fear is that you have much to fear on your own, but as a child of God you have the assurance of his protection. Under his protection bad things may still happen to you, but his love can never be taken away. His love is what sustains you through the worst experiences of life. I can testify to the truth of that in my own life and so can millions of other faithful Christians.

When it comes to fear, trust and hope can't be separated. Trust and you'll have hope. If you want hope, you simply must trust. Trusting in God is the way to overcome fear. The good news is that Jesus helps us trust, just as he helped the man with the sick son overcome his unbelief.

Chapter Seven
Get Past Frustration and Bitterness

~~~~~
=====

*Acrid bitterness inevitably seeps into the lives of people who harbor grudges and suppress anger, and bitterness is always a poison. It keeps your pain alive instead of letting you deal with it and get beyond it. Bitterness sentences you to relive the hurt over and over.*

*Lee Strobel*

For many years I was bitter. I wanted to be married but I wasn't. To the best of my ability, I had obeyed God. I couldn't understand why he wouldn't answer my prayers for a spouse.

One day I looked in the mirror and didn't like the person I saw. I snapped at people who asked why I wasn't married yet. And worst of all, I was sick much of the time and having a miserable life.

To be honest, I can't pinpoint a specific day when that happened, but it was sometime in my forties. I was far from over the hill. Even so, I was old enough to know better. I decided if I wanted to see any happiness in the remainder of my life, I had to let my bitterness go. It was hard. In fact, it was a battle that took years.

You know why? Because I was angry at God. I thought I deserved better and told him so. I had lots of arguments with him but they were remarkably one-sided. He would let me talk (or sometimes shout) myself out until I was exhausted and finally quit.

I made two mistakes. First, you can't argue with God and win. He's always right because, well, he's God. And second, I tried to figure God out. You can't do that either, because, well, again, he's God and nobody can figure him out, even those radio preachers who say he talks with them every day.

Looking back, it all seems pretty foolish, but then much of our lives look foolish in retrospect. We operate from the wisdom and information we have at the time. Usually that's pretty inadequate. God, on the other hand, not only sees the Big Picture but he sees the future as well. He has all the information there is to have. He never makes a wrong decision.

If you're caught in resentment right now, I know how you feel. You believe you have a right to feel that way, and surprise! Maybe you do! The trouble is that it's not getting you where you want to go. You're stuck in neutral, even going in reverse. Every moment lived in bitterness is just that much less happiness you're experiencing. Oh sure, there may be some sad satisfaction about stewing in your own juices, but if you keep it up, where will you be in five or ten years?

One of my goals for this book is to help you quit as much self-destructive behavior as possible. Bitterness falls into that category. As Lee Strobel said above, bitterness is a poison that ruins your health and your outlook on life. It's so deadly it must be one of Satan's favorite tricks.

I mentioned earlier that one of the truths you learn in grade school is that everybody's not going to like you. Add to that the playground lesson that life isn't fair. Oh, it **should** be, and we want it to be, but in the real world, that's not the case. Bad things happen to good people like you and me, nasty people seem to prosper, and justice seems as rare as honest politicians. As Christians, we expect better, all the while knowing that Jesus told us life was often going to stink.

Everybody on this planet wants to have their own way. The problem is that some people will be as cruel and thoughtless as they can be to get their own way, and you've been the victim of that. When they first read the Golden Rule, they stopped after reading "Do unto others..." The world is full of them. Sometimes they're in the role of your boss. Other times they're your boyfriend or girlfriend. They don't care who they step on. To them you're just another rung on their ladder.

Now I'm not suggesting you start acting like them, nor do I think you should build up a thick shell around yourself so other people's bad behavior never hurts you. I do believe we should all acknowledge that these jerks exist so we're not shocked when they wander into our lives. Many of them hide their jerkiness very well. They can be alluringly charming; sometimes we even fall in love with them. But at a certain point their mask slips and they step on you to get their own way.

When that happens, you're angry at them for doing you wrong, but you're also angry at yourself for letting them take you in. Some sort of warning should have gone off inside your brain but didn't.

It may not sound Christian to call people jerks, but let's be realistic. Jesus had the same problem with the Pharisees. They were the worst kind of jerks--religious jerks who manipulated people through fear and guilt. The word "jerk" wasn't around in the Aramaic language then, so Jesus called them a "hypocrites." The Bible clearly tells us there are wicked people in the world. They were around then and still are today. Some folks engage in occasional wicked behavior (we call it sin), while others seem to have a terminally wicked personality. The second kind of people are lost. Until and unless they get saved, they're going to wreak as much havoc as they can because they don't have a conscience.

We singles have to protect ourselves. Sometimes that can be exhausting. It's not unusual to imagine somebody is picking on us at work or in college, because we tend to take upsetting conversations and replay them over and over until we convince ourselves we're a target. That's a real danger you and I need to guard against. Our minds can run wild, especially if we try to figure out other people's motives. Most of the time we don't understand what we're doing ourselves, let alone what drives others.

# Misery and happiness don't mix

One of the stranger facts of life is that all of us do things that are counter to our happiness, and we keep doing them. For example, most of us, at some time, have been envious of married friends. It's natural to see a happily married person and ask, "Why not me?" We wonder why God is favoring them and not us. We want what they have. We covet what they have. Outside of church, you never hear the word covet. The Bible warns us not to covet, but what does that mean, exactly? How does it apply to single people?

Coveting is an intense desire to possess something. God specifically forbids coveting because it almost always leads to bad consequences. Besides not coveting our neighbor's wife (or husband), we are not to covet their material goods.

But is it wrong for singles to covet a happy marriage? Is it a sin to intensely desire a union God himself instituted for our good? We can hunger for God. We can hunger for a holy life. We can hunger for a marriage blessed by God. Many single Christians make the mistake of believing that since they are single, that must be God's will for them, then they start to feel guilty about wanting to be married, because they assume that's **not** God's will for them, or they'd be married. Sheesh!

Determining God's will for you is a very tricky thing. I believe God has specific tasks for us at certain periods of our life. God would not assign you to a task that requires spiritual or emotional maturity you don't yet have. He may want you to do certain things when you're young and have more energy and stamina, and different things when you get old and are not as active. God might want you to be single at a certain time in your life then married later. I honestly don't know whether God wills it for certain people to be single all their lives and others to be married. Marriage is a good thing, but singleness is certainly not a curse or something to be ashamed of. Many saints in the Bible were singles. Jesus was single too.

Coveting or desiring marriage turns into sin when we become envious of our married friends or relatives. Envy contains an element of resentment toward someone who enjoys an advantage we wish we had. It's easy to fantasize about their marriage breaking up so they would be as miserable as we are. It's also easy to become angry at them because they can't sympathize with our problems any more. Even if we never act on such thoughts, they're still toxic because they contain seeds of ill will toward another person.

In your healthy quest for happiness, here's something to remember:

### You can't be happy by making yourself miserable.

It sounds like a ridiculously obvious statement, yet when you think about it, how often do you do things that make yourself miserable instead of happy? Lots! We singles feed destructive emotions like anger, hate, bitterness, fear, envy, and we keep stoking them as if we're building a bonfire.

You can't move toward happiness when you're doing something that makes you miserable. You're going in the opposite direction! You're traveling **away** from the thing you want most.

Usually we're so wrapped up in our emotions that we're unable to be objective, take a step back, and see what we're doing to ourselves. We don't look on envy or bitterness as self-destructive, but taking a step back, it's easy to see they are. At the time, however, they seem like reasonable reactions.

I'm sure you've heard the old joke: "Why are you hitting yourself on the head with a hammer?" "Because it feels so good when I stop."

Being bitter about your singleness is hitting yourself on the head with a hammer. It doesn't accomplish anything. It certainly doesn't take you where you want to be. It only makes you miserable. And remember what we said above: You can't be happy by making yourself miserable.

We like to blame another person or our situation for our misery, but the truth is that we **do** have control over our emotions. Some emotions seem to naturally follow a circumstance: death = grief; loss = sadness; success = happiness; accomplishment = satisfaction.

Not getting what you want = frustration, anger, resentment, bitterness. But does that **have** to follow? Are we locked into our emotions, like a knee-jerk reaction? Are we too stupid or stubborn to see that certain reactions **hurt** us rather than help us? Is it possible to break that equation?

I believe we can, with God's help. We are human beings with a free will, not robots programmed to act a certain way. We can **stop** doing ourselves harm and start doing ourselves good. We don't bring on the justice we crave faster by being bitter. We aren't "entitled" to our resentment.

Why did Jesus command us to love our enemies and to pray for people who use us? Because it **breaks** that cycle of self-destructive emotions. It does the exact opposite of what our mind is shouting for us to do. It replaces hate, something negative, with love, something positive. This was the immense power Mohandas Gandhi employed, and he learned it from Jesus Christ. Instead of hating the British, Gandhi loved them. Instead of rioting against them, he held peace marches and fasts. Their tanks and bayonets were powerless against him. He turned India upside down and eventually won its independence. Martin Luther King Jr. followed Gandhi's example and won the same victory for American civil rights.

## Is bitterness a choice?

You may have read the book *Happiness is a Choice*, by Frank B. Minirth and Paul Meier. It's an excellent book about depression and worth your time to read.

But did you know bitterness is a choice as well? We don't think of it that way because it creeps up on us slowly. Nobody actually says, "I think I'll be angry and bitter for the rest of my life," but that's what many singles do.

I'm not disputing the fact that you may have a right to feel angry when something doesn't go your way. Life isn't fair. We get hurt and something or somebody is to blame. The sad part, though, is when we **hold on** to our bitterness, taking some kind of pleasure in having been wronged. To say we enjoy the feeling may be too strong, but we've all run into martyr types who seem to feed on telling their story then soak up whatever pity their listeners give them. The first time you hear them relate a tale of how they were treated unfairly, it evokes your compassion. The tenth time you hear them repeat the story or tell you their new "story of the week," you have to bite your tongue to keep from saying, "Get over it and move on."

We don't usually recognize a martyr complex in ourselves because we sincerely believe we **do** have a legitimate gripe. Maybe we don't even go around sharing our misfortunes with others. We may just replay them for ourselves, over and over and over. One of the disadvantages of being single is having too much time to think.

No matter what the tragedy is in your life, you owe it to yourself to rebuild and move on. If people can move on after losing a spouse, a child, or a sibling, you and I can move on too. That doesn't mean the hurt goes away. It doesn't mean you're happy-go-lucky again. It certainly doesn't mean you completely forget about it. What it **does** mean is that you choose peace instead of bitterness.

> **Bitterness is a self-imposed state of suffering, a prison cell that the inmate holds the key to. Bitterness is *not* a tribute to the person or job or whatever was lost. It is in no way a noble thing. Bitterness is choosing to prolong pain when you no longer have to.**

I have known bitterness in my own life. I wasted too much time with it because I refused to get over my shock at being betrayed. I was an innocent victim not once but several times, and each time I stayed in my victimhood too long. I was so angry I couldn't let it go. Maybe you know that feeling.

I'm no genius. I'm telling you about my mistakes so you won't repeat them. When you see the foolish things I've done, they can serve as a warning to you not to be as stubborn as I was. My emotions speak strongly to me, as I know yours do to you. They cry out for justice, but when justice doesn't come, we can slide into bitterness, demanding that life should be fair. Even if it's not fair to everyone else, it should be fair to **me**, because I'm different. Sound familiar?

Life is a matter of choices: good or bad, right or wrong, hard or easy, peace or turmoil. In an objective, unemotional state, we think a person would be **crazy** to choose turmoil over peace, but that's the problem. We **are** temporarily crazy when we choose turmoil--bitterness--over peace. We're not acting in our own best interest, even though some loud voice tries to convince us we are. In the twisted logic of the crazy person, we actually **believe** the argument that bitterness is our right. Our **right**? Our right to **suffer**?

When you look at it that way, it seems insane. But when you're hurting so bad you can't think straight, it seems like the only way to go. It doesn't even seem like a choice. It seems like the inevitable consequence of being hurt. Most people indulge their bitterness for a while then do move on and get over it. How long we choose to remain in it depends on each person and their perceived loss.

To drop your grudge and move on, you simply **must** trust God for justice. Most of us want revenge instead of justice. Justice recognizes that we may have had a role in the situation. None of us is perfect, and we all have a hard time admitting we may be some of the cause of our own problems. We are fortunate, however, that God deals with all human beings out of mercy, as well as justice. If he were fair, if he dispensed only justice, none of us would be able to stand before him, including me.

Bitterness accomplishes nothing except self-destruction. When you realize many of your health problems stem from bitterness--headaches, digestive upset, high blood pressure, sleep disturbance--you conclude bitterness is a luxury you can't afford. It has no effect on the person or situation you're angry with, but it **does** destroy your own peace.

When you're hurt or angry, your reactions are not always logical, nor are they in your own best interest. Holding on to an enormous sense of being wronged, you want some sort of payback. The difference between sane and insane people is that sane men and women let go of their anger. They do not harbor it. Insane people obsess over their pain and build on it until they do something horrible or violent.

You and I want forgiveness from God for our own mistakes. We must be willing to let him forgive **other** people who have wronged us as well. We can't expect him to treat our sins one way and the sins of others another way.

Bitterness is toxic in the life of a single person. It skews your judgment, alienates you from others, and brings on a whole host of health problems. It's a matter of survival to let bitterness go. Bitter people can't be happy. Bitter people can't give and receive the kind of love that makes life meaningful. Stop torturing yourself over the injustices that have been done to you. Only as you hand that anger over to God will you be able to laugh and enjoy life again.

# Ruth's lesson for singles

One of the most stunning lessons for singles is found in the book of Ruth, one of the shorter books of the Bible but filled with such wisdom you cannot afford to overlook it.

This book tells of a young woman named Ruth, born and raised in the pagan land of Moab. Ruth and Orpah married brothers, the sons of the widow Naomi. Both husbands died, also leaving Ruth and Orpah widows. There was no one to take care of the three women. As they journeyed toward Naomi's homeland of Israel, Orpah turned back, to stay with her family in Moab, but Ruth stuck with Naomi. Ruth's vow of loyalty to Naomi is one of the most touching passages in all of Scripture:

*But Ruth replied, "Don't urge me to leave you or to turn back from you. Where you go I will go, and where you stay I will stay. Your people will be my people and your God my God. Where you die I will die, and there I will be buried. May the Lord deal with me, be it ever so severely, if even death separates you and me."* *(Ruth 1:16-17)*

Together the two women returned to Bethlehem, Naomi's home town. In ancient times widows had few rights. Without a husband or male relative to support them, they could starve.

Naomi sent Ruth to pick up leftover barley during the harvest. Under Jewish law, landowners were required to leave the edges of their field and any missed stalks for the poor. As Ruth was gathering these leftovers, she met Boaz, the owner of the land. Ruth later told Naomi, who explained that Boaz was a relative of hers. As a distant relative, a "kinsman redeemer," Boaz had the right to marry Ruth to rescue her from poverty.

In buying a piece of land Naomi owned, Boaz also acquired Ruth, who was the widow of Naomi's son Mahlon. Boaz was required to maintain the dead man's name, along with his property. What started as a business transaction turned into love. Boaz was impressed with Ruth because of her loyalty toward Naomi. Boaz and Ruth married, taking Naomi into their home to care for her in her old age.

God blessed them further. Their child was named Obed. He became the father of Jesse, who was the father of David. David, you may remember, was an ancestor of Jesus of Nazareth, the Savior of the world.

This story of Ruth is more than a heartwarming romance. It's an instruction to single people today on how to step out in faith in a godly way. Throughout the incident, both Ruth and

Boaz acted with integrity and in the highest moral character. Times have changed over thousands of years, but finding a good Christian spouse still calls for following God's rules. Ruth was a believer. When she left Moab, she also left her idols behind and took Naomi's God, the God of Israel, as her own. The message is clear: Marry a Christian if you would have God's blessing on your marriage.

We should notice also that Boaz acted with honor toward a vulnerable young woman who was in dire straits. That is a warning to men to treat their date with respect. Christian men cannot give their faith lip service then surrender to their base desires. Likewise, Ruth's behavior was pure. Single women are to carry themselves with dignity and not do anything to lead their date to act dishonorably.

The entire book of Ruth is characterized by kindness: the kindness of Ruth toward Naomi, Naomi toward Ruth, Boaz toward Ruth, and God toward all the people involved. Kindness is such a rare virtue that people are surprised when they receive it. As singles, we become more attractive when we are kind. We can be kind to others because God has first been kind to us.

Finally, the most important lesson from this book is that Ruth overcame her grief over her husband's death and stepped out in faith. Stepping out is the cure to bitterness. Too often we singles become passive, waiting for something to happen. I realize that in our culture, men are expected to ask women out, but when that call doesn't come, what then?

Becoming proactive gives you something to focus your energy on instead of your hurt. What seems wiser: a nonstop stream of negative thoughts about how unfairly you were treated or working toward a goal of a happier life? Goals are energizing. Brooding is draining. Goals give you something to look forward to. Sulking traps you in the past, reliving disappointment, going through the same destructive emotions over and over.

When Ruth left Moab, she left her past there. You and I may not physically change locations, as Ruth did, but we need to leave our miserable past behind and reach out to an optimistic future.

Hope-filled activity gives you a reason to get up in the morning. One of the most important motivators in a single's life is something to look forward to. As you accept life as a challenge and see setbacks as temporary, not permanent, you'll notice a remarkable attitude improvement. A positive attitude can make all the difference in the world.

You can't change your past, but with God's help, you can change your attitude toward it. Once you get over the notion that there's something worthwhile about being stuck in bitterness, you'll find that life begins to open up with new possibilities. I can tell you from experience that self-punishment, namely staying in a place of mental suffering, is not only being stuck but also being self-destructive. If you're a Christian, you're doing a disservice to God and to yourself.

As I've said before, if you can't get unstuck and move ahead, you may need to talk with your pastor or a professional counselor. That's nothing to be ashamed of. In fact, you should be proud that you want to get on with your life.

Our lesson from Ruth is that God stands ready to help his people. He is a kind, loving friend who puts his infinite power at your disposal. God's grace, his unmerited love for you, is one of the most beautiful messages in Scripture. But grace is more than a gift for your salvation. It is the only way to live the Christian life.

# Find hope in God's unpredictability

Over the years, I've learned God can be unpredictable. Every time I thought I had him figured out, he did something unexpected. Oddly, I have found his unpredictability can be a great source of hope.

We often pray for miracles, never expecting God will work in our lives in mundane ways that still achieve spectacular results. If anger and frustration are problems for you, if you've tried to get beyond your bitterness with no success, I suggest you turn it over to God and ask him to work on it. He will require your cooperation, because God never forces us into anything. He respects your free will at all times, even when it breaks his heart.

You may notice a gradual shift in your personality. If you are willing to follow the Holy Spirit's leading, events that used to aggravate you may now seem inconsequential. When you listen to God's promptings, you will choose the better way, the way of love and forgiveness. Over time you will come to see you have much more in your life than your frustration. Opportunities are there, but you can't grasp them if you're clinging tightly to resentment. If you can't recognize that your anger is holding you back, ask God to show you. It may be a frightening experience, but your goal is always to know the truth about yourself.

There's an old saying: "God accepts you just the way you are, but he loves you too much to let you stay there." His goal is to conform you to the image of his son, Jesus Christ. Whatever stands in the way of that goal has to go.

Know that aspiring to be like Jesus makes you a more attractive person. By modeling his love, you will attract love. By living out his compassion, you will find that compassion comes back to you. As you allow Christ to work in you and through you, you will be shocked at the changes. This transformation would be impossible for you to make on your own. Only God can change a life so dramatically, but first you have to relinquish control and follow his lead.

The greatest change from hate to love in the Bible was the conversion of Saul of Tarsus into the apostle Paul. He was a sick, boiling cauldron of rage against the early church, persecuting Christians so wildly he didn't care if his victims died in the process. When Christ struck Saul down on the Damascus road, it wasn't a matter of breaking Saul's will and forcing him to turn around. It was a matter of illumination. Jesus caused Saul to see the truth, and as a lover of truth, Saul had no choice but to make a complete change. The scales that fell off Saul's eyes were symbolic. It was his inner blindness that was healed first.

So it is with us when we give up our resentments and choose to travel God's path. I don't think God's going to knock you to the ground and strike you blind, but the changes he will make in your life can be just as powerful as Paul's.

Life is too short to live it in a constant state of bitterness. You may believe you missed your greatest chance at happiness, but God **is** unpredictable. He will bring great joy into your life if you will let him.

If you want hope for the future, it requires your participation, first in turning your bitterness over to God, then in your willingness to act when opportunities present themselves. You can't let your past poison your future. Learn from my life: Because a romance or job didn't work out before does not mean those things won't work out if you try again. God can give you the courage to try again, and he will also provide the strength you need to pick yourself up time after time.

Life has no guarantees. Just because you follow God is no assurance you will live happily ever after, realizing all the dreams of your youth. But it **is** guaranteed that if you close yourself in and let anger lead you, you will draw **more** unhappiness. This is not the Law of Attraction, Positive Thinking, or some New Age mumbo-jumbo. It's merely the common sense principle that people don't want to be around an ill-tempered person. In the end, it's **your** choice whether you push people away or draw them to you.

Knowing you're right with God gives you a peace that forces out bitterness. Learning to trust God casts the burden of holding a grudge onto **his** shoulders for resolution, and because you love him so much, you're willing to go along with whatever he decides. When you put your relationship with Christ above your personal need for revenge, you have advanced into spiritual maturity.

Yes, God is unpredictable in the way he works, but there are no surprises when it comes to his love for you. God is the supernatural healer who has the power to restore broken hearts. By putting your faith in his decisions for you, you achieve the knowledge that his will is always best, no matter how things seem on the surface. Remember that this life is but an eyeblink compared to eternity. There is a holy justice, and those of us who did not receive it in this life will get it in the next. The hope of heaven is that our tears will be dried and there will be no more suffering--of any kind.

It can be painful to take responsibility for your own life and scary to turn everything over to God, but I did it many years ago and would never go back. I know now that God's opinion of me matters most. My self-confidence comes from his acceptance of me, regardless of my sins. Giving my frustrations from the single life to him has taken a big load off me.

Things may work out for me and they may not. That doesn't matter any more. I believe I am in the center of God's will, and that's what matters. My future is not dreary or hopeless, because God is in charge of it and he desires good things for me.

When you turn your bitterness over to him, you will know the same kind of peace.

# Chapter Eight
# Make Peace of Mind Your Goal

~~~~~
=====

There are many things that are essential to arriving at true peace of mind, and one of the most important is faith, which cannot be acquired without prayer.

John Wooden

We live in a world of noise: television, MP3 players, movies, the Internet, car radio, machinery, cars, trains, and sirens. Then there's the "silent" noise: newspapers, magazines, billboards, store displays, and the glitz of material possessions.

All of these things "shout" at single people in their own way, vying for our attention. It's no wonder when we go to bed at night that we can't sleep. The bedroom may be quiet, but there's too much noise inside our brains.

The Amish think they have the answer to this problem. They cut themselves off from the rest of the world, avoiding the nonstop pull of TV commercials and materialism. Their rules dictate a simple life that hasn't changed much in 150 years. But they have lost a lot of good things in the process. They don't go to college. Many of them don't own cars, so they can't travel far, unless they take a train or bus. They occupy their time by working hard and following rules.

But you're not Amish and you wouldn't want to be. On the rare occasions when you'd like to leave the clamor of the world behind, you wouldn't want to leave it behind for good.

For the most part, it's not the pace of the world we live in that robs us of our peace of mind. It's our thoughts working against us, and they usually fall into two categories: regrets about the past and worries about the future. In this chapter we're going to explore some ways to set your mind at ease so you can navigate through life with an optimistic outlook.

As I said earlier, one of the problems with being single is you have a lot of time to think. If you're able to apply your mind to constructive thoughts and events you're looking forward to, that's a good thing. But if your thoughts have become like little enemies, harassing you to the point you're making yourself upset, it's time to do something about it.

One of the lessons of maturity is that life doesn't turn out as wonderful as we thought it would be when we were young. Looking back, it may seem as if people and circumstances conspired against you to deny you the things you wanted. You didn't get the breaks you expected. Someone in your high school class or the same age as you was more successful. And, as many celebrities have discovered, when success came, a certain disappointment came with it. Either it wasn't as great as they hoped or the elation of it passed too soon. As one professional football player lamented, "Once you've won the Super Bowl, what else is there?"

Regrets over 'What might have been'

Late at night when you're feeling low, it's easy to look back on your life and believe it might have been better if you'd been married, or if you'd married "the one who got away," or if that special person could have appreciated the real you. People who have no regrets are rare.

I used to wonder "what might have been" if this had happened or if that had not happened. It's an interesting fantasy game, but it leaves God out of the equation. God takes a personal interest in each of our lives. He gives us free will to make our own decisions, but in an inexplicable way, he also directs things behind the scenes. We'll only find out in heaven how he orchestrated the events of our lives so certain things happened. We'll find out too, that some of what we considered tragedies in our life were arranged by God with his prime goal in mind: to make us more like Christ.

We're all foolish. The world convinces us its way is best, and for the most part, we believe it. We've been brainwashed into believing fame or wealth brings happiness. We singles believe marriage would give us the ideal life, yet marriage is no guarantee of happiness either, nor is it a cure for loneliness.

Most people put on a pretty good front. Atheists would have us think they live a carefree existence and their secular philosophy provides them with all the answers they need. They may mock Christians about our belief in God and heaven, but the bottom line truth is they have no idea what happens after death. They may argue that Christians trust in fairy tales, yet they cannot prove we are wrong.

Rarely will a rich and famous person come forward and admit their life is hollow, completely devoid of meaning. What they will do is retreat into drugs and alcohol, go to a fancy rehab center, dry out, then do the same thing a few years later.

So take the world's idea of "success" with a large grain of salt. If you think an actor or star athlete or politician is more successful than you, you're only seeing the tip of the iceberg. What's below the surface may be despair.

You can put regrets in perspective by remembering you did not have an owner's manual for your life. You did the best you could at the time with the information and maturity available to you. Yes, we all make mistakes and wish we could redo some bad choices, but God has a way of bringing something good out of the bad, even if we can't see it in this life.

One of the reasons the Jimmy Stewart Christmas movie "It's a Wonderful Life" has been colossally popular for nearly 70 years is millions of people have been disappointed with their life, just as the character George Bailey was. They believe they haven't amounted to much. They have dreams that never came true. They look back on life with regret and think of themselves as a failure.

Let me tell you in the strongest terms I can that God does not see you that way. If you believe in his Son, Jesus Christ, as your Savior, there is nothing you could do to be more successful. Contrary to what the world may tell you, life is **not** a game nor is it a contest. The bumper sticker "Whoever has the most toys when he dies wins" is the creation of a fool.

When you put your life in an eternal perspective, you will see your regrets in a new light as well. Your "might have beens" may bring disappointment, but what truly matters is what will be for eternity. Right now that may not seem to be so. That's all right. Things are not always what they appear. Beyond what we know in this life is a marvelous new world where you will see yourself as you really are. Your regrets and so-called failures will vanish like smoke.

In a perplexing way, Christianity does not make sense. Its truth is so contrary to the world's lies that it's often hard to understand. We are weak yet we are strong. We are poor yet we are rich. We are sinners yet we are saints. We are rejected by this world yet we are accepted in the kingdom of God.

The very disappointments that have so haunted your life have made you precious in the eyes of Jesus because you turned to him in your hurt.

Those regrets that trouble you late at night, those sorrows that prevent your peace are part of what made you the person you are today. When you think you have not become the person you wanted to be, remember that you have become someone much better. Things which would have drawn you away from God have been left behind, burned off like dross when gold is refined.

At some point, each of us has to decide whether we want to keep beating ourselves up mentally or whether we will let it go and trust God to right the wrongs in our life. That's what the Christian life comes down to, because without trust in God, we can become obsessed with the raw deal we have received. We can look for someone to blame, and that's when bitterness sets in. Nothing destroys peace of mind as thoroughly as bitterness.

I recently encountered a newspaper editor who said he enjoyed living in a small town because he was a big fish in a small pond. He had found his place in life and was satisfied with it. If he had worked in Chicago or New York, he would have been just another face in the crowd. We would all do well to imitate his perspective on life. You may not be world famous or even famous in the place you live, but you are famous to the people who know and love you. Even more important, you are famous to God. He follows your every move, not as some fan who admires you today then loses interest and moves on to somebody else. No, to God you are a big fish in a small pond. Your failures and regrets don't cause him to love you any less. He loves you more for surviving them, for being able to look to him for your future. The biggest mistake we singles can make is thinking we've missed out on the best. The best is yet to be!

Whom do you want to please?

One of the sure destroyers of peace of mind is trying to be a people pleaser. Single women can be especially prone to this trap as they struggle to gain approval. I dated a woman years ago who frequently said, "I'm sorry," when she had done nothing wrong. Finally I had to tell her to stop doing that. I'm not sure what was behind it, but I wanted her to feel good when she was with me, not apologetic.

It's normal for singles to replay conversations and events--another hazard of having a lot of time to yourself to think. Many of those reruns involve incidents from work, a popular topic for second-guessing ourselves. While you need to please your boss to keep your job, it's an area that can make you paranoid if you're not careful. Most workplaces have regular performance reviews, but you don't want to wait until then to hear how you've been doing. You can ensure your review will be positive by being absolutely clear on what is expected of you as an employee, then exceed those expectations.

Most bosses don't mind questions. It's smarter to completely understand an assignment and deliver what's expected than to go into it unsure and mess things up. A sign of a competent supervisor is how clear their instructions are. If your boss falls short in that area, don't be afraid to ask questions, even if it upsets him or her. You shouldn't have to take the blame because your boss is vague on what he or she wants done, but in the real world they won't see it that way. You're not a mind reader. If you're not comfortable about what is expected, ask.

Many singles struggle to please their parents. This never ends, no matter how old your parents are, but you can't get so consumed with it that it wrecks your peace of mind. Parents differ on how much control they try to exert on their children. For some singles it can be a real problem. If your parents are controlling and it's ruining your life, the only thing that will stop it is a confrontation. You have to weigh the consequences when you force a showdown, but you also need to envision what your future will be like if you don't.

I went to high school with a boy whose parents imposed impossible standards on him. As a result, he was a nervous wreck thinking he wasn't going to be the best at everything he did. Although he was remarkably intelligent and a gifted athlete, there were times when he failed, and he was crushed that he did not meet his parents' expectations. I lost touch with him after college, so I don't know whether they kept pressuring him as an adult, but it was a sad situation.

In the eyes of our parents, we'll always be their child, but when we become adults, we should expect to be given some freedom to choose our own career and make our own mistakes. The minister at my eighth grade graduation ceremony summed it up well when he said, "It's hell on earth to have to wake up and go in every day to a job you hate." The economy being what it is, some of us don't have any choice. Still, to have your parents force you into a line of work that makes you miserable makes you wonder what their true motives are.

Trying to please your friends can derail your peace of mind too. Whether they become jealous of you if you're more successful, or whether you feel envious if they outdo you, it's yet another potentially upsetting situation. Part of growing up is realizing you are your own person. It's nice to please others and we'd all like that to happen, but sometimes it just doesn't. You shouldn't feel you have to hold yourself back to keep from offending someone, nor should you feel compelled to excel because another person thinks you should.

I don't need to go into great detail about the things men and women do in relationships to try to please their partner. Again, single women seem to be more prone to be people-pleasers than single men do. Only you can decide whether the relationship is unbalanced. Keep in mind, though, that if you seem to be giving far more than you're receiving when you're dating, things will probably get even worse if you get married to a person like that.

Many Christians believe a wife has a duty to be submissive to her husband. Personally, I see marriage as a partnership, with both husband and wife making decisions together. If you are constantly trying to please a selfish person in a dating relationship, you're headed for trouble. That can wreck not only your peace of mind but your health as well. A final note to single women: Beware of trying to "reform" a bad boy or selfish man, thinking you'll be able to accomplish that **after** you get married. You're living in a fantasy world.

As Christians we all want to please God. Surprisingly, you'll never be able to do it by being perfectly obedient. I went through a phase in my twenties when I was so puritanical I wouldn't even go in a tavern to eat because I thought it would damage my reputation.

As a lifelong Christian, I can confidently tell you that **no one** can obey the Ten Commandments. Trying to measure up for God is impossible. **That's why Christ had to die for us.** We can feel guilty, worthless, and like a complete failure, or we can recognize the truth that Jesus was perfectly obedient **for** us, doing what we could never do.

The next time you're distraught over not being good enough for God, remember you're looking to yourself for salvation and not to Jesus. God loves you as you are, accepts you as you are, and takes you from where you are to where he wants you to be. If you're a believer, God looks at you and sees the perfection of his only Son. Jesus' righteousness is your righteousness. Jesus' perfection is your perfection now. You can love God, you can do your best to obey, but when you stumble, it's no longer a matter of not measuring up.

Your acceptance and future are secure in Christ. That's where your peace of mind is too. You have put on Christ, Christ pleases his Father; therefore, **you** please the Father.

Worry: Incompatible with peace of mind

Being single and having a lot of time alone to think, we often lapse into worry. I'm convinced worry is one of Satan's favorite tools because it draws us away from God. Worry is the opposite of faith.

Worry is also a consequence of our fallen nature. It's extremely hard to eliminate, which makes me think it's due to the Fall. Human beings just seem compelled to worry.

Constantly asking "What if...?" destroys your peace of mind. Hidden within that question is the implication that if something bad does happen, God won't take care of you. You're old enough to know that sometimes when you get into a jam, God doesn't bail you out, no matter how desperately you pray. You've already had that happen. That **doesn't** mean God is unreliable, which is what we automatically assume. What it **does** mean is God wants you to turn to him in the midst of your jam so he can see you through it. Most of us don't want to get through it. We want to instantly get **out** of it.

But Jesus never promised us a jam-free life. What he did promise us is that he would never abandon us, that he would stick with us and help us no matter what happens.

My philosophy of life, and I believe it's biblical, is to take all the precautions I humanly can, then trust what I can't control to God. The Bible encourages us to work hard, save money, plan ahead, and be wise in our personal habits.

Let's look at finances, one of the biggest causes of worry for singles. No matter how much money you make, I would recommend you get a reputable financial adviser. Right now you may be laughing, thinking you can barely make ends meet. Where would you get money to invest? That's one of the fallacies about financial advisers. Their job is not to work with only rich people. Their job is also to work with people of modest incomes, to help **make** them rich.

Looking back, I wish I had hired a financial adviser much earlier in life, in my 20s or 30s, instead of in my 50s. I would be much better off today. Investing has become extremely complicated, and a certified financial planner can help you set up a plan to save for your future. This is something very, very few young people do, and let me assure you that when you get old, you will remember my advice and either regret that you didn't follow it or be extremely glad you did.

Saving and investing is something that seems way down the road to most singles in their 20s, but trust me that time passes quickly, and if you put this off too long, you can't catch up. You may also think this is the kind of lecture your parents might give you, and you'd probably be right. But like God, they do things out of love--not to spoil your current fun but to keep you out of trouble in the future.

I wish I could take you forward in time 30 or 40 years. Worrying about whether you'll have enough money is like acid eating away your peace of mind. Crazy things happen with the economy--unpredictable things--but if you have wise, conservative investments, you'll be prepared.

This is something only <u>you</u> can do for yourself.

Don't rely on your employer or the government to provide for your retirement. You're rolling the dice if you do.

Pension plans are fine. Social Security is a good thing. But if you don't start your own personal investment plan in addition to those two things, you are going to run into trouble. This is one of those things you **can** control. Trusting in God is wise, but not planning for your financial future and expecting God to bail you out is foolish.

Everything in our culture screams against saving and planning for your future. Advertisers tell you to get what you want and get it right now. Well of course they do! That means more profits for them. Do you think they care about your best interests? Absolutely not. They use the most sophisticated psychological manipulation in the world to try to get as much of your money as they can, as quickly as they can. Don't be a sucker. Look out for yourself. Your employer's not going to do it, the government's not going to do it, and your parents won't always be around to rescue you.

This is about killing a major source of worry: financial shortfalls. I'm afraid the responsibility is entirely on your shoulders. It's time to man up, or woman up, as the case may be, and do something that at some point in the future, is going to make you absolutely dance for joy that you were so smart.

Hand in hand with saving and investing is avoiding debt. Credit cards may be one of the worst curses ever perpetrated on mankind. I use mine only when I buy things online. Otherwise I pay cash. Do you know why? Because cash is real. Cash is tangible. You can see it **disappearing** from your wallet and you can see that you don't have any more. Yow! No money left! Time to **stop** spending.

You can't do that with a credit card. Credit cards make money unreal. It turns cash into numbers that hardly anybody pays attention to, until it's too late. Then you know what? Your credit card company wants **cash** to pay your debt. You have to put **real cash** into your checking account to make things right.

Call me a dinosaur, but the whole point of banking online, credit cards, and debit cards is to make it **easy** to spend money. When cash, the stuff you work hard for and put up with a lot of abuse for, becomes unreal, becomes just numbers, it doesn't seem as precious.

When you pull out your wallet, count out bills for your purchase and see how few are left, it makes you stop and think. If it's the beginning of the month and you won't have any money left for the next couple weeks, it **really** makes you stop and think.

Avoiding pain: Actions have consequences

Actions have consequences. You may not like to hear this. I expect you're getting a bit angry right now, but my job is not to baby you in this book. My job is to help you **avoid** pain, and worrying is intensely painful. Let's talk about something else that can demolish your peace of mind: health problems.

Too many young singles ignore their health as long as it's going well. They eat whatever they want, and some don't even have health insurance. This is not a popular topic, but some wise decisions now can help you miss a trainload of pain later.

As I mentioned before, I had cancer and radiation therapy when I was 25 years old. I had lived a pretty puritanical lifestyle: I did not smoke or drink alcohol, and I had never used illegal drugs. I did all the right things, medically speaking, but cancer ran in my family. All four of my grandparents had it. Three died from it. My father later died from it. My mother had it twice.

My cancer was something I could not have prevented. However, many kinds of cancers **can** be prevented, or at least you drastically can reduce your odds by taking certain precautions. If you use any type of tobacco product, stop. If you eat an unhealthy diet, at the very least, moderate it. If you don't get any exercise at all, start walking and doing activities to build up your energy level.

When we're young, we feel invincible. We take unnecessary risks and do dumb things, thinking we're going to live forever. But even the simple act of not texting while you drive or not using your cell phone in the car can save your life--and the lives of others.

Listen to this from somebody who knows firsthand what he's talking about: **Worrying about whether you're going to die from an illness <u>consumes</u> you.** It tears up your peace of mind like a mental chainsaw. It fills your waking hours; it keeps you from sleeping at night. It drains you of physical energy as if you'd been digging ditches all day.

That's why it's incredibly important to take care of your health, no matter what age you are. Look around you. Look at people on walkers, carrying oxygen tanks, in nursing homes before their time.

If you have your health, you have everything.
If you lose your health, daily living becomes
a miserable chore.

We take our health for granted when we're young. I know I did. But even so, I have never used tobacco, drunk alcohol, or used any illegal drug. I believe the good health I enjoy today is a result of denying myself those things when I was younger.

Be smart. *Please.* Be smart early in life. Go to your doctor for regular physical exams to catch any problems early. Conscientiously go to the dentist. Take care of your eyes as if they were your most valuable possession--because they are.

It's self-defeating for us singles to become hypochondriacs, running to the doctor every time we imagine we have some deadly disease, but a sensible balance is to educate yourself on the warning signs of various illnesses, then go for regular exams to monitor your body's systems. It's always wiser to prevent health problems than to let them go and try to fix them later.

As I said earlier, take all the precautions you humanly can, then trust the rest to God. I suffered a second bout with cancer seven years ago, 34 years after my first incident. But because I go for regular exams and had a doctor who was monitoring my health carefully, my prostate cancer was detected and treated early. Today I am cancer free.

I cannot waste my life worrying about whether cancer will return again. I do everything I can from a medical standpoint, then I trust the rest to God. I have to, or I would drive myself crazy worrying.

The big worry: Ending up alone

Finally, we singles spend a lot of time worrying about ending up alone. Some of us will end up alone, but contrary to what many singles believe, it is **not** the worst thing that can happen to a person. The worst thing that can happen to you is ending up with someone you don't want to be with.

When I was in my 20s and 30s, getting married was the most important thing in my life. I thought about it constantly, I talked about it constantly, and naturally I prayed about it constantly. It never happened.

At some point I learned the difference between solitude and loneliness. I still get lonely at times, but I also appreciate the constructive time I spend alone.

If you worry about ending up alone, the time to do something about it is **now**. Online dating did not exist when I was young. Even so, it is filled with dangers. Many people online are not who they claim to be. Still, some singles form meaningful relationships and do marry people they met through the Internet.

People can get married at any age. Occasionally you'll read about a couple in their 60s or 70s getting married. Good for them! To set an age limit on marriage restricts your chances. Who knows? You may find the right person later in life and decide marriage is a good choice.

Marrying later may avoid many of the petty arguments of a young marriage. When both partners are emotionally mature, they realize lots of minor differences are not worth fighting about. They are more accepting, overlooking the small idiosyncrasies we all develop over time.

Do not let any pastor, especially a married pastor, convince you that people who are married are specially blessed by God and single people are somehow cursed. That kind of misinterpretation of the Bible has caused more harm to Christian singles than almost anything else. I do not know whether it was God's plan for me to remain single. I know that I am single today, and when I get to heaven, I will find out the reason for it. Some things are beyond figuring out, no matter how much time we spend thinking about them.

Instead of worrying about ending up alone and losing my peace of mind, I concentrate on daily growing closer to God. For middle-aged and older singles, that can melt away much of the stress and bitterness we might feel.

I have older friends who have never married who are happy with their lives. They stay active and involved with people. More than anything, though, they have learned to appreciate their solitude. If you believe you could never, ever live alone for the rest of your life, you will be surprised what maturity does to you. I felt that way for a long time too, but as I've grown older, I have become comfortable with the person

I am. I am not afraid to spend time by myself. I have many interests and hobbies. I see life as an ever unfolding adventure.

No longer do I worry about what God thinks of me, because I finally understand that he loves and cherishes me and someday will bring me back home to live with him forever. That is the essence of peace of mind. No matter how turbulent the circumstances around us, that is the eternal, unchangeable truth.

Self-esteem and peace of mind

Somewhere we got the idea that peace of mind is acquired passively, that if you just meditate or open yourself to it, peace will come. That's not true. Since all the things that destroy your peace of mind are active and forceful, you have to meet them with a stronger force. That stronger force is the power of the Holy Spirit, working in and through you.

To get the calmness you desire, you have to put God in charge of your mind, and you have to do something most people find very difficult: Trust in God. Many of your mental distractions come from attacks on your self-esteem, real or imagined. When you get your self-esteem from your own accomplishments, you are going to flinch when someone criticizes them, like your boss. When you get your self-esteem from your appearance, you will have doubts when you encounter someone more attractive than you are or your looks begin to fade with time. When you get your self-esteem from your possessions, you eventually learn that the merry-go-round of buying more and better never stops, and you can't keep up any more.

When the lights are out and your home is quiet at night, do you review what happened to you on the job, especially the things that upset you? We singles can vent to our friends or parents, but it's hard to just let it go.

If these negative mental movies are spoiling your peace of mind, the solution is **not** to try to stop thinking about them through sheer willpower. The solution is to **substitute something constructive**. If the way to stop a bad habit is to replace it with a good habit, the way to sap the power of the endless replay is to think of something that makes you feel good instead. It might be how you can improve a process or procedure at work. Or even better, you can plan your next vacation or an event that you will look forward to.

Your mind will try to fight you on this. It will keep returning to the unpleasant incident and soon you will be inventing a little scenario about what you **should** have done or **should** have said. While there's a perverse satisfaction in being the director and star in these mental videos, the result is that they keep you riled up. What's over and done is over and done. You can't change it with your little mental video.

The important thing to understand with mental replays is that every time you rerun them, you hurt yourself again. You want justice. You want to be treated fairly, but sometimes that doesn't happen and there isn't a thing you can do about it. Now that may stink, but Jesus warned us the Christian life would not be easy. Look at it this way: Forgiving someone and moving on is like taking a sharp pebble out of your shoe. Continuing to think about the insult is like adding **another** sharp pebble every time you replay it.

Get your self-esteem from God and God alone. This is where your true worth comes from. Once you grab onto that truth, nothing can damage your self-esteem. In the end, it is God and only God who counts. His love for you never changes, never weakens and is impervious to any kind of attack on you. You will go a long way toward peace of mind when you can rest in God's love and know you are all right.

You are accepted. You are free. You can relax because God's love for you is not based on your achievements, so you can stop striving. You are fine with him just the way you are.

In the final analysis, you have to be willing to accept the peace Jesus offers you. Worrying and remembering slights rejects that peace. The peace of God demands that you trust in God. That's a tall order, but anything worthwhile requires an exchange. God's peace is free, but you have to give up your bad mental habits to receive it.

It's a choice. Do you want to keep agitating yourself by what you're thinking, or do you want to calm yourself by what you're thinking? You **can** have peace of mind if you choose thoughts that bring peace instead of turmoil.

Chapter Nine
See Faith as Key to the Single Life

~~~~~
=====

Basically, there are two paths you can walk: faith or fear. It's impossible to simultaneously trust God and not trust God.

Charles Stanley

Faith matters so much in the single life that it makes the difference between being contented and being miserable.

That's a big claim to make. For many of us, faith is a nebulous thing, a vague subject we read about in the Bible and agree with in principle but that's hard to pin down and even harder to put into action.

Today's culture erodes your faith. Bit by bit, the claims of science, the acceptance of immoral and even evil behavior, and the general downward spiral of society make people of faith feel like loners. For us singles, our culture makes our problems even worse.

Without faith, we give in to temptation, and there is no shortage of temptations out there. The struggling single asks, "What's the use?" When a crisis comes up, they lapse into fear.

Most of us are not faithless, but we are struggling. Maybe our faith has been tried and found wanting. Many years ago, my own faith became weak because of too much disappointment. I fell into that "What's the use?" attitude. I had hoped and been disappointed so many times I quit trying, thinking every new opportunity would simply be a repeat of the past. Burned-out faith can turn into cynicism.

Yet if faith is so crucial, how do you get it? How do you restore it if you have lost it? And how do you build it so you can rise above discouragement when things don't go your way? How can you become like the long-suffering Bible character Job?

> *Though He slay me, yet will I trust Him. (Job 13:15, NKJV)*

This is the kind of faith singles need for the long haul, the trust in God that will carry us through this life and into the next. It's not just for saints. It's for everyday, struggling Christians like you and me. This faith empowers you to overcome the world because it comes not from *you*, but from *God*.

Let's explore this all-important element that gives hope to hurting singles. We'll look at what you should put your faith in, and the biggest myth about faith. We'll try to answer the question of whether God owes you a spouse. We'll discuss how to stay faithful when your prayers are not answered. Finally we'll examine the biggest faith question of all: how to trust that God does what is best for you.

What you should put your faith in

If you're going to ask someone for help, it makes sense to choose someone with enough power to get the job done. The obvious choice is the omnipotent God.

Simply put, nothing has more power than God. Nothing is bigger than him, stronger than him, smarter than him. His power has no limits. He is the best and there will never be anyone or anything better. He's not called the Supreme Being for nothing.

God created the universe by speaking it into existence. He alone has the power to create something out of nothing. The laws of physics obey *him*, not vice versa. He has the power to suspend those laws and do whatever he wants.

When the world cannot explain God's actions, it calls them miracles. More often, however, the world wants you to believe there was some logical, natural explanation for the things recorded in the Bible. Recognizing miracles would lead to recognizing God. The world doesn't like that.

Don't be fooled. The human race has achieved some remarkable accomplishments, from electronic wonders to awesome medical cures. But God is real and he is more powerful. Jesus Christ quietly did things science cannot duplicate today. With only a touch, he healed blind people and lepers. He fed thousands with just a few loaves of bread and a couple small fish. Jesus raised people to life who had been dead for *days*, not minutes.

God is powerful and worthy of your faith. We think the government is powerful or our employer is reliable. Then we see them fail and we realize the world's idea of power is meaningless compared to God.

It's easy to get confused. When God does not act, unbelievers accuse him of being weak. They say he cannot be counted on because the situation overwhelms even him. But we must not mistake God's *refraining* to act with an *inability* to act. We cannot always understand God's reasons, but that has no bearing on his power. The existence of the universe proves how great his power is.

The Bible is an account of God acting in the world with power. He still acts today, even though we do not always recognize it. Christ's resurrection from the dead was a shocking demonstration of God's power. You can have faith in his might and his ability to do amazing things. When God chooses to exercise his power, nothing in the universe can stand against him. Christ defeated Satan at Calvary. Nothing stands in the way of God.

Not only is God the ultimate power, he is sovereign. God is in total control. Again, unbelievers would have us think the existence of evil proves God is *not* in control, but to give us complete freedom to love or reject him, God permits people to sin. God does not force people to love him. He did not create human beings as robots, without free will. If God stepped in and prevented sin, all sin, our unbeliever friends would not enjoy him preventing *their* sins. As much as they scorn God, they love the fact that he gave them freedom to reject him.

If God were not in control, the universe would be in chaos. Scientists like to credit everything to gravity and nature, but who created gravity and nature? The universe and planet Earth are intricate systems. Do they merely keep going with no correction, no guidance?

The Bible shows us God is in control. Across thousands of years, God manipulated empires and circumstances to bring about one event: the death and resurrection of his Son, Jesus Christ. Christ is the center of all history. Before political correctness came along, mankind began measuring time from the year of Christ's birth. The most important event that ever happened in human history was the sacrifice of Jesus for the sins of the human race, and God the Father orchestrated every bit of it. Yes, God is in control.

People jokingly refer to God as "the man in charge," but it's true. Nothing happens without his direction or approval. Because the world is stained in sin and evil things occur does not mean God has lost control. Freedom for people is part of his plan. It's a mistake to blame God for the sins of men.

When you have a complaint with a business, you go as high up the corporate ladder as you need to in order to get it solved. There have been times when I have written to the CEOs of companies to get satisfaction, and it worked. You can take your desires, your requests, your hopes no higher than God. He is at the top.

Such control shows not just power, but care. Again, unbelievers may blame everything from natural disasters to mass shootings on God, but the world was essentially ruined when sin came into it. All creation was affected. The nurturing environment depicted by the Garden of Eden became hostile.

When Christ returns, God will remake heaven and earth, as prophesied in Revelation 21:1. Everything will be totally right once more, forever. Our all-powerful God makes his plans come to pass because nothing can stop him. God owns the universe, governing it for his own purposes. It makes sense to put your faith in the One who is in control of everything.

Exploding the biggest myth about faith

If faith in God is a key element for living the single life, then the logical questions are "Where does faith come from? How do we get it?"

Somewhere we got the idea that we can create faith on our own. Your sinful nature tries to convince you faith is yet another work you can produce by trying harder. Maybe if you pray more, go to church more, do more good deeds, read the Bible more... The common thread in all those actions is *more*.

But faith doesn't come from doing more. It's a gift from God:

Let us fix our eyes on Jesus, the author and perfecter of our faith, (Heb. 12:2)

Did you get that? Jesus is the author--the originator or creator--of our faith. *That's* where it comes from. Jesus constantly builds it, refines it, polishes our faith until it gets better and stronger. It's true, however, that we can ask for *stronger* faith, as the man did who begged Jesus to help his unbelief.

As you put your faith in God, your trust is rewarded. Of course that doesn't mean you will get everything you pray for. You will have disappointments when your desires don't match God's will for you. In times of trial, however, God always stands with you to bring you through. God *is* trustworthy.

Trusting God is the great adventure of the Christian life. Far too many singles give up on God because they have been disappointed in the past, but the issue is *not* whether God gives you what you want, but rather whether he is conforming you to the image of his Son, Jesus.

Should we singles stomp our feet, throw a tantrum and tell God, *"I want what I want, and I don't care what you want for me."*? Or do we say, *"My goal is to be more and more like Jesus, and I trust that whatever you allow or don't allow in my life will move me closer to that goal."*

That is submission to God. *That* is how your faith grows, but what a hard road it is to travel. When we singles can be content with what God gives us rather than what we demand, we're on the right path. That's what Jesus meant when he said we each have to take up our cross and follow him. The cross is self-denial. The crown is doing God's will.

Old, mature Christians seem to have strong faith in God no matter what happens to them. How do they do it? How do they stay loyal to a God who denies their prayer requests and allows all kinds of suffering in their life?

They have unshakable faith in God's *love* for them.

Over a lifetime, they have put their faith to the test. They are wise enough to understand that it's not the easiness of their life that matters, because God never promised anyone an easy, painless life, but it's God's *presence* that does.

As I move toward that goal myself, I am often tempted to give in, but a good kind of stubbornness keeps me going. Maybe that stubbornness is really my faith in disguise, implanted in me by the Holy Spirit. We are not always aware when the Holy Spirit is working in our lives.

Stumbling through the troubles of the single life, you and I keep going, when by all human explanations, we should have given up years ago. The believer who is self-aware realizes he or she is not continuing in their own strength. God is moving them along. This is putting your faith into action.

I had trouble with this until I recognized God's love for me is an indisputable fact. It is true **no matter what happens to me**. Humanly speaking, that doesn't make sense. We judge another person's love for us by how they treat us.

We judge God's love for us by what he allows or doesn't allow in our life. If we suffer or don't get what we want, we assume God doesn't love us. If we go through one hardship after another, we think God is either punishing us or doesn't care about us at all.

These expectations are produced by our sin-ruined world. Continually fed TV commercials promoting immediate gratification, we carry that attitude into our personal lives too. Prosperity gospel preachers prey on this presumption: God loves you and wants to shower you with all kinds of material blessings to prove it.

Well--no!

You can twist the Bible to make it prove almost anything, and they have. They proof-text verses about the abundant life and conclude love equates with receiving good things. But what if it doesn't?

God doesn't want to turn you and me into spoiled brats. Nor does he want us to see him as a cosmic vending machine: Insert donation, receive blessing.

Instead, he wants to build our Christian character, and that takes faith on our part. We're so stuck on our worldly assumptions about love that we can't fathom God could be different, and better.

God wants to build an intimate relationship with you. He doesn't want you to build an intimate relationship with the *stuff* he gives you. We are to worship the Giver, not the gifts. Worshipping anything other than God is idolatry.

If you have faith in material gifts instead of in God, you overlook the many spiritual gifts he provides:

- **Salvation**, the greatest gift in the universe;
- **Jesus Christ**, your gift in heaven, with his unlimited love;
- **The Holy Spirit**, your lifelong counselor here on earth;
- **Baptism and the Lord's Supper** to strengthen you;
- **Forgiveness of sins** every time you ask;
- **Material blessings** like food and shelter to keep you alive;
- **Family and friends** who make life so much happier;
- **Work** to contribute to society and make you feel worthwhile;
- **The beauty of creation**, including nature and pets;

- **Individual talents and abilities** that give you joy.

Poor people can be happy; rich people can be sad. Single people can be happy; married people can be sad. Faith in God makes the difference. Your time on earth is short. When you judge by appearances, you will bog down in discouragement, but when you put your faith in God's love for you, you have something solid to hold onto no matter what storms rage around you.

Maybe your faith is very small right now, microscopic, in fact. Maybe life's twists and turns have left you feeling cynical too. You may be asking yourself, "What's the use?" Here are some ways you can open yourself to God increasing your faith.

Ask God to help you forgive the people who have hurt you. We often have expectations of others they could never live up to. When you think about your own shortcomings, it helps you identify with what's going on in other people's hearts. They're struggling, just like you are. They're uncertain. They do things to try to make life better for themselves, but sometimes their actions cause hurt to others. That's called sin, and we all do it. All of us, at times, have selfish streaks. Sin can have painful consequences, not only for the sinner but also for the people around him or her. We try to rationalize our own sin, but deep down we know we did wrong. In the Lord's Prayer, Jesus commanded us to *"Forgive us our trespasses as we forgive those who trespass against us."* You and I have received Christ's forgiveness from the cross. That obligates us to forgive others who have hurt us. When you forgive, you open your heart to God's faith-building power.

You can remove another roadblock when you forgive yourself. We singles can fall into the habit of focusing on our faults, exploding them out of proportion, then going over them again and again. Soon we can't see any worth in ourselves at all. But the second greatest commandment is to love your neighbor *as you love yourself.* God *wants* you to love yourself, with a healthy, realistic love. He wants you to understand your worth comes from *his* love for you, not from anything you accomplish or don't accomplish. Part of loving yourself is forgiving yourself. You're not perfect and never can be. Confess your sins to God and as he forgives you, forgive yourself too. When you love yourself in a healthy, godly way, your faith *will* increase.

Last, the best way to open your heart to stronger faith is to go back to God in prayer. Prayer is hard. It feels unnatural. As proud human beings, we don't like asking anyone for anything. We'd rather do it ourselves. But that's not how God operates. He *wants* you to depend on him. In fact, the more you depend on him, the better he likes it. Have realistic expectations of God, though. Don't treat him like a genie, asking him to grant your wishes. I had to learn the hard way-- through having my prayers denied--that God is more interested in making us become like his Son Jesus than he is in making us successful, rich, or famous.

Don't buy the pitch of the Prosperity Gospel you hear on TV. Don't believe God wants you to be successful. Some of God's greatest saints were poor and unknown. Instead, ask God for understanding and wisdom. Ask him for humility. Ask him to help you love others and be more compassionate. When I asked God for those things, he granted my prayers. Understand that being more like Jesus makes you successful in God's eyes, and his opinion of you is the only one that really matters.

Having greater faith is possible when you let God do the heavy lifting. You don't wind up faith, like you wind up a clock, then have to wind it up again when it runs down. Remember this: The Holy Spirit living within you is where faith comes from. *He* provides it. *He* generates it, and *he* strengthens it when needed.

Does God 'owe' you a spouse?

The biggest test of our faith as singles may be our response when God does not provide us with a spouse.

Is that a legitimate request? Of course! Old Testament women prayed for children. Why shouldn't we feel confident in asking for a godly marriage? When it comes to prayers being answered, God looks at our motives and whether our request is what's best for us.

For many years I was angry with God because he gave me neither a spouse nor an explanation. I was left single and confused. Maybe you feel the same way.

We will understand some things only in heaven:

- Why are some babies born disabled?
- Why are some Christian people ill most of their lives?
- Why are parents killed in tragedies, leaving their children orphans?
- Why do innocent children die?
- Why do the wicked prosper and the good suffer?
- Why am I single?

These big questions of life are unsolvable mysteries for human intelligence. Sadly, they cause many people to lose faith in God.

When singles reject God because they are not married, they are valuing the gift over the Giver. They have turned their desire for a spouse into their god, placing more importance on it than on their heavenly Father.

Is that why God doesn't grant some of us a happy marriage? I honestly don't know, but I can tell you *I* have been guilty myself of valuing marriage over God.

Let's face it. It's depressing to see nonbelievers enjoying what seems to be a happy marriage. We feel marriage is a reward, a gift God should bestow on *his* people, not on those who have no time for him. After all, shouldn't there be rewards for following Jesus?

That belief creates another trap: following Christ because we expect something in return. It's yet another form of the Prosperity Gospel, believing God "owes" us something. Especially in the United States, we talk about our rights so much we feel we're entitled to much more than we are. In reality, God doesn't owe us a thing. Salvation, and everything else God gives us are *gifts*, not rights.

It took me years to get over the idea God owes me a spouse simply because I'm a Christian, but I cannot claim any credit for changing my own mind. The Holy Spirit corrected my thinking, gradually revealing his will for me through the Bible.

I realized, after many years, the greatest good for me, the thing God had been trying to give me all the time, was *himself,* not a spouse. I had thought the love of a wife would be more real than the love of God, but I was wrong.

Let me be clear:

**I did not stop *wanting* a spouse,
but I *did* put that desire in its proper
perspective.**

Many pastors make the mistake of saying that all singles need is God. If that's true, those pastors should never have gotten married in the first place. God should have been enough for them.

When we understand this problem properly, it redirects our faith to *God*, not to what he gives us. We should love God for himself, his holiness, his kindness, and because he loved us first. Our relationship to him is child to Father. Children receive gifts from their parents, but they have no right to make demands on them.

The greatest gift God has given us is salvation. Any blessing on top of that is also a gift, not a right. We do not have the *right* to a spouse. It is a mystery why some people receive certain blessings from God, a mystery I believe we cannot understand in this life.

How to stay faithful when your prayers are not answered

Recently I read a book about prayer in which the author said if you meet all God's requirements and claim his promise in Scripture, you could be *guaranteed* your prayer would be answered.

I have not found that to be true in my life, and I'll bet you haven't either.

Maybe there's a loophole. Maybe I did not completely meet the requirements of perfect holiness and obedience. Considering my sinful nature, it is impossible for me to do that. Come to think of it, it's impossible for *any* human being to be perfectly holy and obedient.

Unanswered prayer has probably caused more singles to become disillusioned than any other problem. If you cannot put faith in your prayers, does that mean you cannot put faith in God, who answers prayers?

People have been debating this question for centuries. If the answer lies with God's will, then what about requests that are biblical and worthwhile, like getting married?

Human beings cannot know what God knows. For reasons clear only to him, he has not helped me find a wife. I will understand those reasons only when I get to heaven. But what about more pressing needs, like those of the parents of a dying child or a person who needs a job or thousands of people asking that their country be spared of war? What happens when legitimate prayers like those are not granted?

As we scratch our heads and make judgments about God's character, we can only conclude some areas of life will remain mysteries, beyond our understanding. We know sin has effectively spoiled the world. That's part of it. We know God's plans are massive and inscrutable. That's another part of it. We know we cannot order God about, like a genie. That's yet another part.

Taken together, those parts are still inadequate. They do not satisfy the "why." They leave you as confused and powerless as before. In the end, you have to separate the *process* of prayer from the One who answers--or does not answer--prayer.

You can put faith in God, but not necessarily in your prayers. Even when you believe you are asking within the will of God, you may get a "no" answer or an answer that leaves you saying, *"But that's not what I asked for."*

For me, trusting God has meant I will take whatever he gives me, understanding he knows what is best for me better than I do. He knows the future. He knows my flaws. He knows how I fit into his plans.

That does not mean my prayers are half-hearted. I still pray with passion. I tell God this request is important to me and why, even though he already knows. I try to make my case, as weak as it sometimes is. In the end, however, I ask rightly if I put my faith in God and sincerely say, "Not my will, Father, but yours be done."

Our culture has conditioned us to want what we want and break our backs trying to get it. How many times have you heard some starry-eyed person say, "Anything is possible?" Thanks to too many Disney movies, we singles expect our lives to turn out like a fairy tale. We may be grown-ups, but we still believe in happily-ever-after.

I do not put my faith in happily-ever-after any more. I do not find anything in the Bible or my own observations about life to support that fantasy. Instead, the realistic approach is that of Paul:

> *I know what it is to be in need, and I know what it is to have plenty. I have learned the secret of being content in any and every situation, whether well fed or hungry, whether living in plenty or in want. I can do everything through him who gives me strength.*
> *(Philippians 4:12-13)*

It takes real spiritual maturity to be content with what you have. It takes letting go of disappointment and the feeling you have been cheated in life. *After all, I am a good person and deserve to live happily ever after, don't I?* we ask.

Well, in real life, very few of us, good or bad, get what we deserve.

Now this would be a very depressing fact except for one thing. *Christ* is the gift, not what he does or doesn't give you. Only by putting God in his rightful place can you avoid that feeling of being cheated. As we saw earlier, anything you give more importance to than God becomes *another* god, and you know what the First Commandment says about that.

The happily-ever-after syndrome is just a variation of the "American dream," in which a person rises from rags to riches, has a perfect family, buys a mansion and expensive cars, and becomes a success story everyone admires. Sure, people may achieve those goals, but should they be what a *Christian* aspires to, especially a Christian single?

Don't get me wrong. I believe in dreams. I think goals and hopes are necessary. They give us purpose in life, something to get up for in the morning, but the key is to have *godly* goals. Otherwise, like many celebrities who find themselves rich and famous but empty inside, you set yourself up for crushing disillusionment.

The only way to guarantee living happily-ever-after is by having *eternal* life--and that is only possible through Jesus Christ.

Then, if your dreams do not come true in this life, they certainly will in the next, when you are reunited with God. Our existence on earth, which seems so solid and real, is like the blink of an eye compared to the life to come. We are creatures caught in time, unable to comprehend eternity, where there are no clocks or calendars.

Eternal life starts *now* for those in Christ. Put your faith in *that*. Know that if your aspirations are currently frustrated, the happily-ever-after you dream about will still come to pass. You cannot know what God has in store for you in heaven, but even being in his presence will be joy such as you have never known on earth. Whatever hole you have in your soul right now will be filled to overflowing when you meet Jesus face to face. *That's* the happily-ever-after. *That* is your dream come true.

When your prayers are not answered, you can put your faith in the truth that Jesus lives. That rock can never be shaken. It is repugnant to the secular world yet is the centerpiece of our faith. In the first century, Paul wrestled with that skepticism. Christ has indeed been raised from the dead, Paul said, and our faith is *not* in vain.

What does this mean to single Christians? It proves our faith in God is warranted, and along with it, our faith in his Word. This world, on the other hand, wants us to put our faith in self-indulgence. Christ has different values: purity, honesty, integrity, kindness.

When you know Jesus lives, it sets off a cascade of confidence in your life. The way is clear and you are on it. What you believe in has meaning. Jesus Christ has been tested by time, and you will not have to readjust ten or twenty years from now, as if you had put your faith in some passing fad.

What's more, Jesus Christ is the highest good because he is God. What is the highest good every person most desires? Love! The apostle John tells us where to find that highest good:

God is love. Whoever lives in love lives in God, and God in him. (1 John 4:16)

That is a shocking statement. Watch a few music videos and you'll think love is sleeping with someone you are not married to. Watch a TV commercial and you'll believe you can love a car. Have you ever noticed that so many of the sources of "love" you hear about require you to spend money?

Putting your faith in the resurrection of Christ and the truth that God is love anchors us singles. This truth gives you an unimpeachable reality on which to ground your life. By definition, there can be no disillusionment when you know the Truth. Other, secular "truths" may be disproven or become obsolete. Christ never will. What's more, God's love is the standard for comparison. Every other love, no matter how intense, pales when you compare it to God's love for you.

Yes, we are creatures of flesh and blood, convinced that the touchable is reality and God is faraway. We seek the touchable in the here and now. We hunger after the physical and material, and plenty of merchants are eager to help us get it.

Perhaps the greatest irony of life is that the *seen* is illusion and the *unseen* is real.

God is worthy of your faith, and as impossible as it seems, he *loves* you passionately. Most of us have put our faith in a very attractive person and later found out they did not love us. But God tells you through his Word, over and over and over, that he loves you and will *never* leave you.

Wouldn't it be silly to have a crush on a celebrity? He or she wouldn't give you the time of day. But God, the most important being in existence, loves *you*. He loved you when you were in your mother's womb, and he loves you today in spite of your flaws and shortcomings.

God zealously wants you to spend the rest of eternity with him. That's why he sacrificed his Son Jesus, so you can come home to him in heaven. That was an agonizing price for God the Father and Jesus to pay, but they both did it willingly because of their great love for you.

Single Christians need to live in this love. Depression comes easily. You can feel worthless, as if no one wants you. But feelings are not facts. On the contrary, the most precious love in the universe is yours for the taking. You can depend on God's love.

I have always drawn my self-esteem from the truth that God loves me passionately. The love from human beings is fickle. They can be pledging their undying loyalty to you one minute and showing you the door the next. When things go wrong, and they often do, you can grab onto God's love for you like a life preserver. In fact, it is.

If you are the type of person who feels confident only when you are in a romantic relationship, change your focus to the love *God* has for you. Does it matter what the world thinks of you? Does it matter that you are in your forties, fifties or sixties and never got married? What matters now and what will matter through eternity is *God's* never-ending love for you.

So much of life is silliness. Striving for fancier cars, bigger houses, prestigious titles--it's like chasing after the wind. The well-lived life has nothing to do with how much money you make. It's about honoring God and treating others with love. In the Almighty's eyes, the person of modest income who lives for Christ is far more successful than the most famous billionaire.

The older I get, the more convinced I am that the greatest treasure any person can possess is the sacred love of God. Even though I do not believe "Jesus is your husband" if you're a single woman or "Jesus can meet all your needs" if you're a single man, I *do* believe single people commit a tragic mistake when they undervalue the love of Christ. In my own life, it has had such wonder-working power I could not have survived without it. When I ran out of strength, Jesus's love for me empowered me to go on. When I was in the deepest pit, it pulled me out. It even has the stunning ability to heal a broken heart.

Never make the mistake of judging God's love for you based on whether your prayers are answered exactly as you want. When I heard doctors say, on two separate occasions, 'You have cancer,' I didn't give up on God. When I prayed I wouldn't get laid off but lost my job anyway, I did not doubt God's love for me. Even when I prayed about promising relationships and they fell apart anyway, I never lost faith in God's love for me.

Maybe you pray and feel as if your request goes no higher than the ceiling. Don't be deceived. I cannot explain all the reasons God allows bad things to happen to those he loves, but I can assure you it grieves him as much as it does you. God is not uncaring. He wants you to depend on him, the more the better. He has an incredibly complex plan for humanity and somehow you and I are part of it. When you realize the Creator and Sustainer of the universe is deeply in love with *you* even in the midst of your unanswered prayers, it's a mind-boggling thought. Nevertheless, it's true.

Faith trusts that God does what is best for you

When you're going through the worst times of your life, you would naturally get angry if someone told you God is giving you what is best for you. God allows pain and suffering to come into our lives. On rare occasions, he even disciplines us to get us back on the right path. Suffering is one of life's great mysteries, but I don't have the wisdom to answer the 'why?'. I only know it helps if we keep in mind this life is not all there is. There is a heaven where suffering and pain do not exist.

That's the real problem, isn't it? We want to be in control, but we're not. A mature relationship with God sees him as your heavenly Father and you as his child. In the ideal father/child relationship, which this is, the father is wiser and more experienced than his child. The perfect father makes correct decisions and the child, knowing this, obeys.

Our Father may be perfect, but none of us is a perfect child. Tainted by a fallen nature, we want our own way. Often when we pray, we're sure we know better than God. It sounds funny on paper, but that's how it is. We're disappointed or angry when we don't get our way, which is understandable considering our emotional makeup.

Faith in God has to ignore what our emotions tell us. Very often, God's ways don't seem logical to us. They seem to be the opposite of what common sense dictates. Look at Joshua marching the Israelites around the walls of Jericho. How absurd! The army inside the city must have gotten a good laugh over that. Never had a city been conquered by just marching around it. When Jesus came to the tomb of Lazarus and asked that the stone be rolled away, the people told him Lazarus had been dead four days. Dead is dead. Death is final. There was nothing anyone could do about that.

It took me most of my lifetime to let God be God. I too wanted a genie I could order around, materializing whatever I wanted, including a wife. I still struggle with accepting God's answers to my prayers. Sometimes I'm so sure that what I'm asking will be the best thing for me or for the person I'm praying for. When the opposite happens, when God answers *"No,"* I don't know what to think.

Faith that God does what is best for you is not a matter of giving up, but it *is* a matter of surrender. Giving up is not caring any more. Surrender is coming to the realization that since God knows best and has my best interests at heart, it is wiser to accept his decisions. Let me tell you, that's still hard. I still care. I still get upset, but a lifetime of experience has taught me that I'm not as smart as I think. And I'm certainly not smarter than God.

The Bible is jam-packed with people who thought they knew better than God. They disobeyed him, they defied him, they even sneaked around thinking they could get away with sin and he wouldn't find out. Their stories are a catalog of misery. God forgives sin, but the consequences of sin are always bad, not good.

Those examples are in the Bible for us to learn from, but thick-headed, rebellious children that we are, we think our situation can be different. We think God will change his rules for us. Or maybe, like driving over the speed limit on a deserted country road, we think we can get away with it and nobody will notice. Satan wants us to believe God has an indifferent attitude toward rebellion. There is no example of that in the Bible.

I believe God treats our disappointment with grace. He understands our sinful nature better than we do and is forgiving of it. God isn't going to change his ways just to give in to our selfish desires. He is committed to doing what is best for us even when we can't understand it. A loving father knows that a child without discipline and boundaries is headed for trouble.

We Christians are more than willing to trust completely in God for our salvation, but suddenly we get cold feet when it comes to trusting him to run our life. It never strikes us that God is trustworthy in *all* things, not just one aspect. The good news is that if we ask sincerely, God will not only increase our understanding of his ways, but our faith in him as well.

Just as we singles will struggle with sin all our life, I believe we will struggle with faith too. We make fun of "Doubting Thomas," who had witnessed three years' worth of miracles as one of Jesus' apostles, yet he refused to believe this same Jesus had risen from the dead. If anyone should have had strong faith, it should have been Thomas. His story was included so we may learn from it.

Sometimes what's best for us hurts. Is it best for you and me to be single? It sure doesn't feel that way. Is our singleness God's will for us? I truly don't know, and I have given this decades of thought. There is a whole host of suffering on earth. Theologians tell us God doesn't cause suffering but he does allow it. Much smarter people than I am have tried to figure out why.

Faith in God has to believe in his goodness even when our eyes seem to show us the reverse. Job's wife told him to *"Curse God and die."* (Job 2:9) Yet Job held onto his faith in God through one tragedy after another. Job refused to let the circumstances of his life dictate his image of God. That's faith, the kind of faith we singles need.

You and I have to trust in God and his goodness no matter how things seem. Your emotions may tell you to "Curse God and die" but your faith tells you to trust God and live. The God who paid such a terrible price to save your soul is a God who loves you immensely. That kind of love wants only the best for the loved one. Despite your doubts, you know deep in your heart that's true.

Chapter Ten
Use Hope to Rise Above Your Hurt

~~~~~
=====

Godly hope is the energy of life.
Rev. Percy McCray Jr.

Some of us singles will get married. Some will not. Life is full of mysteries, so I can't explain it.

Most of us learn at a young age that we're not going to get everything we want in life. Others knock off one success after another, and it's much later before they run into something they just can't have, no matter how hard they try.

This is a hard lesson to learn and can drive you into bitterness if you're not careful. The wise single person constantly guards himself or herself from going down that path. Sadly, I took a detour into bitterness and it was many years before I managed to pull out of that quicksand and back to a hopeful attitude. I believe God extended a hand and yanked me out.

Just as a disabled person has to accept their limitations, so do single people. My father was disabled from stepping on a German land mine in World War II. The injury to his foot prevented him from doing some things, but not from having a happy life. I was fortunate to learn that lesson from him. Now don't get me wrong: I don't equate singleness with disability, but it **does** impose limitations on us.

Within the church, an unspoken prejudice has arisen against single people. Most pastors don't know what to do with us. Although there is no biblical foundation for it, these pastors imply that being married is more godly than being single. Maybe it's because we singles are not adding to the flock. Or maybe it's a mistaken notion that marriage is God's will for every Christian. Just looking around would tell them that's not true. They would also be forced to admit marriage is no guarantee of happiness. If it were, there would be no need for all those marriage conferences. Some Christians stick it out in miserable marriages. Christians get divorced at the same rate as nonbelievers. Nobody ever went into marriage thinking it was going to be a lousy time.

I can tell you one thing for sure. It's better to go through life with a hopeful attitude than feeling hopeless. How can singles stay hopeful in spite of what life throws at us? How can you stay hopeful if you'd rather be married? And finally, how can you be hopeful if you believe God has let you down?

Treat every day like a mini-life

We singles fantasize about the future and have regrets about the past but forget that we can only live in the present. We can't change what has or hasn't happened to us yesterday. We may not even have the ability to control what happens to us tomorrow. But today is a different story.

The beauty of living in the moment is it's more manageable. It's easier to have a happy day rather than a happy life. If you put enough happy days together, you **will** have a happy life. When your strength is running low, it's more doable to have a positive attitude one day at a time. By now, you know I believe in learning from your past and preparing for your future, but our actual living is done today.

When you see each day as a mini-life, you get a brand new one the moment you get out of bed in the morning. If yesterday stunk, so what? You have a brand new chance today--a brand new life today. Every day brings new opportunities. As you grow wiser, you'll learn to *make* opportunities, not wait for them to come to you. While today may be your mini-life, you have the extraordinary blessing of doing things that will make tomorrow's mini-life better.

Seeing each new day as a mini-lifetime helps you stay hopeful. It's a shorter haul. It takes less energy than looking miles and miles down the road. It also helps you appreciate small things more. If it's beautiful weather today, that makes a big part of a happy day. If it's nasty weather, well, it's only for today. Tomorrow may be better, but even if it isn't, it's only for a day, that day. If you have a place to live and food to eat today, those are two big things to be thankful for. A nice meal takes up a decent amount of your mini-lifetime. You can be happy during that part of it, even if the rest of the day was rotten. Your mini-lifetime can be made right by a small pleasure, like your pet or a favorite TV program or a good book. If you have a hobby or something to look forward to tomorrow, the happy moments can erase the negative parts of your day. Make it your goal to go to bed hopeful about what a fresh tomorrow might bring.

Our lives turn into drudgery when we stop being grateful. It's helpful to compare your life to others who are not as fortunate as you. Rather than make you feel guilty, it should cause you to appreciate the good things you *do* have.

Every single should have something to look forward to tomorrow, no matter how small or inconsequential it may seem. When you stop finding pleasure in things that used to interest you, it's time to see your doctor or a professional counselor about depression. Sometimes medication is the answer. Sometimes talk therapy helps. If you're a single parent, you may find it hard to make time for some small pleasure for yourself every day, but it's an important part of your emotional health.

Living in the present brings a certain sharpness to life, a fine focus that may be missing if you're not as mindful. You need to be aware of the consequences of your actions--some things do have an effect on your future, but concentrating all your energy on today makes current happiness more attainable.

> *"Therefore do not worry about tomorrow," (Jesus said) "for tomorrow will worry about itself. Each day has enough trouble of its own." (Matthew 6:34)*

The 16 or so hours you're awake every day present a fresh possibility of getting what you want out of life. You don't have to repeat yesterday's failure today. If you try something different and approach your goal in a new way, you'll make some progress. Thomas Edison didn't consider the thousands of unsuccessful attempts to invent a light bulb failures. He thought of each one as a success, because it eliminated one possibility and brought him another step closer to his goal.

Enthusiasm is in short supply for some singles. When you only have to generate enough enthusiasm to last 16 hours at a time, it's much easier than working up enough for the entire rest of your life. Instead of taking the easy way out, the way of defeatism, you can, just for today, put in the energy to be positive. After all, what has negativity gotten you in the past? Only bad consequences. Since it doesn't work, why keep repeating it?

Expecting good things in your mini-lifetime puts you in a receptive mood. Your confidence will impress others. They'll notice a new, improved you. I don't believe in the Law of Attraction, but I do believe that faith in God opens your life to his blessings. By praying new prayers for different things, you may be surprised at what you get.

You can see clearer in the mini-lifetime of today. The consequences of your actions may be instant or they may occur in the near future, but doing small things right can produce big results. Whether it's getting out a stack of paperwork or doing the most unpleasant jobs early in the day, you'll be able to take immediate pride in your accomplishments, which stokes up more enthusiasm for the rest of your day.

Knowing God is helping you brings hope. Part of an intimate relationship with Jesus is sensing his approval on work well done. When you give your employer your very best, you set a high standard for yourself. Knowing you did the absolute best you could makes each mini-lifetime a success.

When you grow tired of waiting

Hope increases when you have something definite to hope for. Millions of singles wait their entire life for the right person to come along. Let's look at it from a familiar perspective. Have you ever been out of work? Did you just sit home, waiting for an employer to find you out of the blue, then recognize what a great worker you are? No! You replied to ads, you mailed out resumes, you knocked on doors, you networked, you went to an employment agency. You got in-your-face aggressive until you landed another job. You went about getting a job as if it *were* your job.

If you want to get married, desperately want to get married, you may have to practice that same kind of aggressiveness. "But that's not me," you may say. Well, has what "you" are been working so far? Einstein said the definition of insanity is doing the same thing over and over and expecting different results. Has waiting gotten you the results you want so far? No? Then it's time for something else: action.

The law of averages says the more potential spouses you meet, the better your odds of getting married. But quantity isn't necessarily quality, so it's important to do some screening *before* you go out with anybody who is breathing. Don't expect to find a potential Christian spouse in a bar. That weeds out that scene. The booze-and-dim-lights crowd is usually interested in something else. You'll be as out of place there as one of those folks would be in your church.

Online dating is a good way to pre-screen candidates but with one major warning. Single women tell me dating web sites are full of players, men who lie on their profile and are looking for somewhat naive, desperate girls. These men are just bar lizards who have expanded their hunting grounds. If they lied on their profile, it may not become immediately obvious, so be cautious. Protect yourself! Use common sense and every instinct to keep yourself from getting into a dangerous situation.

Blind dates usually strike a note of horror in singles, but they do have the advantage of being pre-screened by a friend or relative who sets it up. First, the person doing the matching should know both of you fairly well. Second, the matchmaker should genuinely care enough about both of you to not set you up with someone who is obviously wrong. And third, the matchmaker should be mature enough to not get offended if the two of you don't hit it off. If he or she accuses you of being too picky, remind them you want to get married only once and you want it to last the rest of your life. This is not like picking out a new bowling ball.

Speaking of matchmakers, in larger cities there are professional matchmakers who pride themselves on getting people together for marriage. Yes, they're pricey, but they're also good because their reputation can depend on word of mouth. What's more, they sincerely enjoy their work and take great pleasure in matching a happy couple. Marriage is the best kind of testimonial they can get.

Don't overlook amateur, unpaid matchmakers. Some women at your church, someone at your club, or a friend of a friend may be one of those souls who has a knack for bringing the right people together. It may not be scientific, but sometimes it works.

Another interesting tactic is to talk to as many married couples as you can and find out how they met. You might hear some creative ideas you can work into your own search. It will also give you hope that if they can do it, you can too.

It's a very touchy point, but some singles could stand to do a little work on the outside, even if their insides are fine. One of the painful truths of life is that especially with younger singles, physical attractiveness is an important factor. That may explain why diet books sell so well. I see nothing wrong with having cosmetic surgery, if it improves your self-confidence. Tattoos? You'll have to decide for yourself if that's objectionable, but I think it's true that the more tattoos a person has, the more they limit their job opportunities.

Many singles, both men and women, take a sort of perverse pride in their sloppiness. *"That's who I am!"* they proclaim, unwilling to change for anybody. Really? Then don't expect a knockout to come begging you to marry them. It's not going to happen.

This emphasis on physical attractiveness may be off-putting, but it's a reality you have to deal with. If your feelings get hurt because you can't be accepted as the "real you," remember that we either have to adapt to reality or be strong enough to go it alone. I refuse to compromise on my Christianity, but changing some other things about myself is not as important.

The more options you have to meet marriageable people, the greater your hope will be. If one avenue doesn't work out, maybe another will. There's an old saying that "God can't steer a parked car." You have to *do* something to get results. When you turn getting married into your life-project and carry out active strategies, you're helping God by doing your part.

Looking on marriage as something you "hope" happens some day is not the right attitude. That's as passive as being out of work and saying you "hope" a job comes along some day. There's a fine line between aggressiveness and desperation, it's true, and needy or desperate women scare men off like the plague, because a man is afraid of being smothered by a woman like that. Many Christian men sincerely want to get married, but like all men, they worry about losing their independence. They want a wife who will be a partner, not a nag, a companion, not a clinger. I don't envy the delicate dance women have to do with a nervous man, but I think the best approach women can take is to show such a man that you are his friend first, someone he can feel more comfortable with than anyone else. It's very difficult not to try too hard when you find someone you love, but friendship clears the way for mutual understanding.

Stepping out in faith is especially difficult if you are, by nature, a shy person. The situation feels threatening because you are haunted by past embarrassments. To overcome your shyness, you must compare your life as it is with what you would like it to be. So far, hanging back and being shy have not gotten you what you want.

Being aggressive may take nothing less than a complete personality overhaul for some singles. As you learned in the chapter on shyness, this may have been a convenient excuse in the past, but you need to abandon things that aren't working. If you're a single woman, consider this. Many

Christian men are shy, having been rejected in dating. There's absolutely nothing wrong with them except they've been burned in the past. They may need an assertive, friendly woman to get the relationship started. Likewise, if you are one of those shy men and you meet a woman you'd like to ask out, ask God for the courage to step out in faith. If she says no, you'll be no worse off than you were. If she says yes, though, it could change your life forever.

We singles often underestimate ourselves, but what's worse, we underestimate the power of God's help. We also exaggerate the degree of hurt we might feel if things don't work out. You're stronger than you think, and after all, in the Holy Spirit you have the best Comforter on earth.

All the while you're waiting, the clock is ticking, the calendar is turning, and months have a way of turning into years. You need to put yourself where eligible mates can be found and you need to make yourself as attractive as possible.

In our stubbornness, we sometimes demand that a potential mate takes us as we are. That's understandable with our Christianity, but we can't be as uncompromising on other things. It may be painful, but if you're really serious about getting married, you might ask your best friend to tell you about your habits or personality traits that are scaring potential mates off. You may be completely unaware of them. Let's face it. Our Number One Priority in life is to allow God to conform our character to that of his Son. The more you do that, the more attractive you become as a person, too.

Who of us couldn't stand to be more kind or considerate? Who of us doesn't need to be more willing to overlook others' minor flaws? And is it necessary to be right all the time or to give another person a piece of your mind?

We singles can become pretty independent. We can develop some bad habits. To say, *"That's just the way I am,"* is not a legitimate excuse. If you're a sincere Christian, you should be open to chucking those abrasive personality traits. They're not doing you any good and they could be standing in the way of the things you want most in life.

The Christian life can be painful at times, but with God's guidance and support, it *is* doable.

God can turn your life around in an instant

One of the most exciting aspects of being a Christian is knowing God can turn your life around in an instant. This is a constant source of hope for single people.

The most astounding example of this in the Bible is the resurrection of Jesus Christ. When Jesus' lifeless body was put in the tomb, his disciples went into hiding, afraid they might suffer the same fate. Their dreams of a conquering Messiah were smashed. Once again the religious leaders and the mighty Roman army had triumphed. Hope was gone.

But when you are a loyal follower of God, things are not always what they appear. Conquering the Roman army had never been Jesus' purpose. He would do something that would make a bigger difference--a life and death difference--for every person ever born. He conquered sin and death. Seeing Jesus alive, healed, risen from the grave finally drove home to the apostles that this was a power that could do things that had never been done before. *"All things are possible with God,"* Jesus had told them earlier (Mark 10:27).

You'll find countless cases of people in the Bible having their lives changed in an instant: Joseph being in prison in the morning and being in charge of the entire land of Egypt that same night; Gideon hiding in his wine press and being turned into a mighty military leader; Jairus the synagogue official mourning his dead daughter, then watching Jesus raise her back to life; Mary and Martha weeping over Lazarus then unwrapping grave clothes from their live brother; Paul being the meanest attacker of the church, then being struck down and turning into its greatest missionary.

Every day you get out of bed and face life with hope and faith in God is another opportunity for things to turn around for you. Some changes will be small, some will be staggering. You have probably experienced these gifts from God. They drop into your life so unexpectedly that you know there's only one place they could have come from: your loving heavenly Father.

Hoping in God for things to change is different from other hope for two reasons. First, God is all-powerful and can do anything, and second, God is sovereign and in control.

When your life is troubled, you may feel as if God is absent, but that's your emotions talking, not the truth. And when tragedies happen, we can't understand them. We can't make sense of why a loving God would allow such horrible events, yet our lack of understanding doesn't change the sovereignty of God. God is in control, regardless.

Every word in the Bible is there for a reason. The stories of miraculous rescues are there to give you hope.

What we sometimes miss in those stories is that the people cried out to God for help. Sometimes they prayed for years before that amazing turnaround happened, but when God acts, he can act very quickly.

Your prayers may take half a lifetime for God to work out. It also may take years to prepare you and other people for the opportunity. God's timing is right. We are anxious, thinking if we don't get married or reach a goal by a certain age, we will never have another chance. God is not only the God of second chances but of *many* chances. If he thinks it is right for you, he will present another opportunity.

You can pray for your needs with confidence because Jesus said you can. You should not make *demands* on God, but as his beloved child, you can make *requests* because of the family relationship you enjoy with him. Jesus intercedes for you as your brother and great High Priest. If your prayers are selfish or amiss, Jesus makes them right before he takes them to the throne.

God's sovereignty means he is in control of everything. Imagine the intelligence, the planning, the power that go into orchestrating seven billion human beings. Yes, everyone has a free will and can choose their actions, but God can also work with those actions so his will is carried out. None of us have the ability to understand it, but for the Christian, there is no such thing as coincidence. The Bible shows God intervenes in the lives of his people.

While it may *seem* things happen abruptly, years, perhaps decades of intricate planning went into that moment. Singles must be ready to take advantage of opportunities when they are presented. That's one of the reasons it's so important to be well-read in the Bible. When you already know God's laws and what pleases him, you don't have to go hunting for an answer. That's not to say you shouldn't consult the Scriptures when a vital decision confronts you, but being prepared helps.

- **Hope** is believing God has an alternative plan.
- **Hope** is believing there is more than one perfect person for you if the "right one" gets away.
- **Hope** is believing that if marriage doesn't happen, you can *still* have a happy life. God has indescribable ways of changing both you and circumstances if you are willing to surrender to his hand.

Being a Christian puts you in the body of Christ, the fellowship of believers who love one another. As you pray for others' needs, you may ask them to pray for yours. Some of the most wonderful answers I've had came when I prayed for others. I think God must take special delight when we reach up to him in this way.

If you want to be married, don't be embarrassed to ask others to pray for you. United praying is more powerful. If God will grant the request of one of his children, it multiplies that when several pray for the same thing.

What is the Christian's true goal?

Single people have many goals, perhaps foremost to get married and live a happy, God-honoring life. Since God instituted marriage in the Garden of Eden, that's certainly a worthwhile goal, something you should feel no guilt aspiring to.

If you search the Bible, however, you will not find marriage as your uppermost goal as a Christian. You'll find the answer from Jesus at the conclusion of the Sermon on the Mount:

> *"Be perfect, therefore, as your heavenly Father is perfect." (Matthew 5:48, NIV)*

Obviously, it's impossible for human beings to be perfect, whether they are Christians or not. So what did Jesus mean? What does he *really* want you to do? There is only one way you can be perfect: through the perfection of Jesus Christ himself. When you are born again, the righteousness of Christ is credited to you. When God the Father looks at the Christian, he sees his Son, who shares perfection with the Father and Holy Spirit.

As hard as you may try on your own, you can never achieve holiness for very long. Your sinful nature gets in the way. But Christ's holiness is imputed to you.

**The only way you can be perfect is by putting on Christ.
That is the true goal of the Christian.**

The Christian life is one of struggle against your own sinfulness and the lures of the world. It's too exhausting to live on your own. You simply *must* have the constant help of God.

Fellow Christians understand this. Through our own failures, we have learned the futility of trying to be sinless. You can't earn your salvation on your own, but to the best of your ability, to honor Christ for his priceless gift to you, you *can* strive to obey. You *can* keep the Commandments as well as is humanly possible--which is not perfectly.

When you surrender your life to Christ, serve others, and do your best to obey God's laws, you become an attractive person. Although your first priority is to Jesus, a side benefit is that you may draw the attention of another Christian who admires your walk with God. A sincere life partner will be drawn to someone who is equally serious about their relationship with Jesus Christ.

You can't be a genuine Christian without loving God and loving others. Such an attitude of selflessness makes you someone worth spending life with because the qualities of Christ will shine through you. If you make Christ your true goal, good things are bound to follow. People are hungry for love. They will be drawn to you to the degree you are drawn to Christ. I'm not suggesting you strive to imitate Christ for selfish motives, but if your intention is pure, if you're doing it for Jesus' sake, out of love for *him*, unexpected blessings may follow.

Allowing God to transform your character into that of Christ is a lifelong project. You may go for years without any conflict. Doing God's will may fall into place quite neatly, then suddenly a hard choice will come up. What you want to do will oppose God's laws. Being human, sometimes you make right decisions, sometimes you make wrong ones.

Never believe that taking a detour will end God's plan for you and that you can't get back on the proper path. You shouldn't indulge in sin or disobedience, thinking beforehand that God will always welcome you back, but when you come to see that you have done something not in his will for you, you should believe repentance and forgiveness are possible. God is bigger than your mistakes. He is able to adjust to your foul-ups and can alter his plans to bring you where he wants you to be. Just as taking a detour can waste time while driving, it can waste time in life. None of us can avoid the consequences of our actions.

Serious Christian singles appreciate the fact that some activities are out of bounds if we would be conformed to the character of Christ. You can't have it the world's way and Jesus' way at the same time. When you sin, you can't expect anything good to come of it. It may be the world's way for a couple to live together without being married, but it isn't God's way. The world may approve of promiscuous sex, but God does not. Substance abuse and materialism are common in our society, but they were never part of the character of Christ.

We single Christians are tempted to believe we're missing out on all the "fun" nonbelievers are enjoying. If you get frustrated enough or angry enough because you're not married, it's easy to rationalize that you have a right to live the same way nonbelievers do. *All* of us rationalize our sins. Thinking it's "now or never" ignores Christ's command that some things should never be in the lives of his followers, no matter what their age.

Joshua permitted no confusion as to responsibility:

> *"But if serving the Lord seems undesirable to you, then choose for yourselves this day whom you will serve, whether the gods your ancestors served beyond the Euphrates, or the gods of the Amorites, in whose land you are living. But as for me and my household, we will serve the Lord." (Joshua 24:15)*

Make no mistake. Today's gods of immorality, sensuality, materialism, and covetousness are idols just as much as those ancient false gods. At some point you have to choose whom you will serve. Conforming to the ills of this world will ultimately bring misery. Conforming to the character of Christ will bring hope.

Have something to look forward to

Conforming to the character of Christ is your first goal and a challenging one, yet you need other goals as you navigate through the single life. You need something that builds your talents, a quest that puts to use the unique gifts God has given every believer.

You can serve God in many ways, but not everyone is called to full time Christian service. You still have to provide for yourself. You need something that brings you fulfillment. If you don't get it on the job, you have to pursue it elsewhere. In fact, it's often wiser to find fulfillment elsewhere, because that may avoid the politics, backstabbing, and jealousy of the workplace.

Having a goal separate from work gives you something personal to look forward to, something that can stay with you if you change jobs. A worthwhile project, something that's fun, helps keep life in the proper perspective. Whether it's learning to play a musical instrument, mastering a craft or art skill, or simply traveling to interesting places, it should match *your* interests and bring you joy.

The single life can be an arduous journey. By having something to look forward to, some reason to get up in the morning, you'll make your life richer. You won't spend spare moments brooding about why you're not married. You won't develop a victim complex. Instead, you'll be actively involved, moving ahead, growing into a happier person.

The great heroes of the Bible were usually portrayed from a spiritual perspective, because the Bible is God's Word, intended to teach us how to relate to him. For us, however, life involves more than just the spiritual aspect. You can still keep your spiritual goal in sight while following other passions. Much of the fascination of life comes from the intriguing people you encounter along the way. It's a privilege to touch the lives of others, as well as an opportunity to spread Christ's love.

Think of the people who have inspired you. Try to be one of those kind of people to others. Jesus did not live his life as a hermit or in a vacuum. You get practice conforming to the character of Christ in your daily life by exercising patience, showing kindness, and listening with compassion. Every day you are presented with a choice of responding to a situation as *you* would or as *Jesus* would. Over time, as you let God guide your life, the difference between the two will disappear.

Hope in God and in heaven

Whatever you hope for in life, know that the *source* of your hope is God himself. All good things flow from him.

Our frustration comes from the difference between what we want and what we receive. Throughout this book I have encouraged you to be proactive when it comes to your heart's desires. The Bible urges us to trust entirely in God, yet nowhere does it tell us to sit, wait, and do nothing while we are praying. Countless examples in Scripture show people trusting in God then acting. Noah trusted God while he built an ark, but when the flood came, he and his family got into that ark. God dried up the Red Sea so his people could flee, not so they could wait on the bank while he destroyed the Egyptian army. David trusted God while he ran from Saul for 13 years, but he still ran.

**It is not a slap in God's face to *do* something
while you are trusting in him.**

We need hope to get us through this life. The most miserable people on this planet are those who have given up hope. Don't let yourself become one of those. The beauty of Christianity says because we have Jesus, we always have hope. Your hope is in him and his faithfulness, not in yourself and your abilities, the government, your employer, or other people.

It can come as a shock and disappointment to learn God's greatest desire for you is *not* to make you happy, but to conform your character to that of Jesus. Ironically, that *can* make you happy if you let that become your greatest desire as well. When you understand that becoming like Christ is life's pinnacle, you will experience deep inner joy as you approach that mark.

To do that, you have to re-prioritize your own desires. That is the biggest challenge for a Christian single because it means surrendering what you want for yourself and wanting what God wants for you instead. That decision can be heartbreaking. I believe that is what broke Jesus' heart in the Garden of Gethsemane.

At the same time, acceptance of God's will brings unparalleled peace. The struggle between you and God is over. Now, that's not to say God will refuse you those things you most desire. Sometimes all he is waiting for is for you to make that commitment to him. If your surrender is sincere, it will no longer matter to you whether you get your own desires or not. The peace is there.

> *"Delight yourself in the Lord and he will give you the desires of your heart." (Psalm 37:4, ESV)*

Some translations interpret that verse as saying, "Find your happiness in the Lord..." Whichever makes more sense to you, see that the implication is when you seek the Lord *first* and wholly, you will either realize God was your true desire all the while, or God will reward your surrender by giving you the other desires of your heart. Either way, you can't lose.

This verse is a stark reminder that choosing God's will for yourself over your own desires is *not* the same thing as giving up on life. In fact, it's just the opposite. When you surrender to God, when you "delight" yourself in him, you open the way to getting the desires of your heart. This is the ultimate act of trust, the submission of *your* will to your Father's will.

I said at the beginning of this chapter that not every person gets married. Some singles will get married then will divorce or be widowed and will not remarry, spending the rest of their life single.

Along the way, whether you marry or not, your toughest task will be to not give up hope. If you hope in marriage for your ultimate happiness, you may encounter a disappointment that is unbearable. But if you hope in God, you will make it through life, trusting in his love for you.

You can't hope in God without also hoping in heaven. Heaven is where God lives. Jesus spoke of it often, and he never lied. If he told us heaven exists, it does. If he told us it is a place of peace and joy, it is. If he told us that believing in him will enable us to join him in heaven after we die, we can accept that as a fact.

Heaven is not a fairy tale land nor is it a place of clouds and harps. Little actual description is given of heaven in the Bible, but we do know spending eternity in the loving presence of God will be an experience that cannot be described in words.

You should not view heaven as a consolation prize for people who do not get married, but for what it truly is: the realization of the true desires of your heart. I'm not even sure what the true desires of my heart are. They are so deep and hidden I can't understand them. But I *do* know one of them is to be loved for who I am, to be unconditionally accepted, with all my faults and failures. Heaven is the place where that will happen.

Since I was a small boy, I have believed we come from God and we will be happy only when we return to him. We are all homesick for heaven, whether we recognize it or not. Many of the yearnings we experience on earth are our desire for God, but we mistake them for something else. We try to force the square pegs of success or fun or possessions into the round hole in our heart when only God will fit it perfectly. The deepest desire of my heart, and yours too, is to be home again with the God who created us.

We are strangers here. Earth can be enticingly sweet at times, but it is not our true home. There's always a disillusionment to remind us there is some place better, and we come from there.

Many Christians believe that in that better place, marriage will cease to exist because we will all be "married" to Christ:

> *"At the resurrection people will neither marry nor be given in marriage; they will be like the angels in heaven." (Matthew 22:30)*

Personally, I believe this quotation from Jesus is open to another interpretation. In heaven we might be like the angels, neither marrying nor being given in marriage, but on the New Earth, marriage *may* be possible. Jesus also said, *"with God all things are possible."* (Matthew 19:26, NIV)

One of God's purposes for marriage was procreation. All angels were created at the same time, as spiritual, emotional, and mental adults. Angels never married to produce more angels. Their sole purpose is to love and serve God. Humans were also created to love and serve God, but we have other purposes as well.

God values love higher than anything else. His two great Commandments are to love him and to love our neighbors as our self. I can't believe that married couples who cultivated a lifelong love relationship will not be able to continue that same relationship after death. I also can't believe that singles who missed out on a love relationship like that on earth will be denied it after death. Will our needs and desires change after we get to heaven? Will Christ satisfy all our needs there? No one, including pastors and theologians, really knows for sure.

Neither can anyone tell you what rewards will given to believers in heaven. The Bible does not describe them. But is it so far-fetched to think singles who were faithful to God in this life will be given a happy marriage as a reward in the next life? Considering the graciousness and generosity of God, it seems very likely! And considering the omniscience of God, our marriage partner would be perfect for us in every way--a *true* soulmate.

One thing is certain. Heaven will be a place of surprises. If the disabled will be made whole, and the old will be made young again, why wouldn't the single be married? When we have resurrection bodies, will we stop being human? Jesus still retained his human body, although glorified, after his resurrection. He ate, he touched his disciples and they touched him. Will we lose the very human desire for intimate companionship in marriage?

When I hear a married pastor say, "Jesus can fulfill all your needs," I want to ask him, "Then why did you get married?"

The idea that Jesus would fulfill all our needs after death is inconsistent with us having a resurrected, glorified body. What will we use that body for? Yes, certainly to serve God, but angels serve God and they have no bodies, unless they come as messengers and assume human form.

The New Earth will be a physical place, this earth recreated. Doesn't it seem logical that in a physical place, we will have physical bodies with senses so that we may enjoy it and function in it?

Let's not sell God short. Let's not underestimate his generosity. Married people, especially married pastors, may belittle our desire for marriage, saying we should be deliriously happy with Jesus alone in the next life, but the fact of a resurrection body on a New Earth implies we will be doing something besides using our voices to sing praise songs 24/7/eternity.

Don't get me wrong. I don't want to downplay the best aspect of heaven: union with God forever. God is the essence of love, the overwhelming love none of us have known on this earth. His perfect love will make us perfect in heaven. We will reach a height of contentment beyond our expectations, yet in the incredible realm of God, it will somehow keep getting better and better. As our sins and selfishness are left behind, we will be freed to love God as we have always wanted but were unable to in this life.

First and foremost, heaven will be about getting God. We reach for him now in our fumbling, bumbling way, with inarticulate prayers from a mind that wanders. We sing in church in our off-key voices. We long to hug Jesus and be hugged by him. Our relationship with him in heaven will be more than the culmination of all we desire.

The Bible tells us God is the light of heaven. His illumination will explain all the hurts and heartaches of this life, the reasons for our trials, and the poignant way he maneuvered our life to make us who we are and to bring us back home. Our anxieties will vanish in a heartbeat. The insecurities that have tortured us for a lifetime will be wiped away with one gaze from our Savior.

God is real and heaven is real. Christ is the shepherd who leads us there. When John said, *"God is love."* (1 John 4:16), he explained the reason for the creation of the universe, including you. Imagine a love that made you, solely because he wants to love you forever. Because God loves you like this, you have hope.

God's love for you began before you were born and will never end. You don't have to wait until you get to heaven to receive it. When you let God be God, when you let *him* be in charge instead of you, you'll realize God *does* know what's best for you, and that's a sure sign of his love. Open yourself to God's love today--right now. Appreciate how God has provided for you in your life up to now. Know that he will be with you every moment, guiding you into the future he has planned for you.

In closing, I admit some of the things I've presented in **Hope for Hurting Singles** will be hard for you to accept. I know that's true because I didn't want to accept them myself when I first learned them. But there's no need for you to go through the same misery I did. You can test these truths yourself. You'll find they work. I hope they help *you* in your journey through the single life.

As long as you hope in God, he will give you the strength you need to face whatever happens to you. Lean on him and your life will be more joyful. Trust him and you'll do less worrying. Talk to him and you'll turn loneliness into solitude. Read his Word every day and you'll gain a new confidence about life.

Just because you're single doesn't mean you're alone. Jesus Christ is your constant companion. He will remain your friend and Savior if you get married, loving you and helping you until you leave this life and meet him face to face in the next life.

We singles have a tendency to be hard on ourselves, judging ourselves by the world's twisted standards, but in God there is hope, genuine hope. Because God loves you so, every new day is a cause for new hope. You never know what can happen. Blessings can shower down on you like a sudden rainstorm.

Look for God in your life. Ask him to show himself and his love to you. Be expectant and hopeful, for the best is yet to come.

Find rest, O my soul, in God alone; my hope comes from him. (Psalm 62:5, NIV)

About the Author

~~~~~

Jack Zavada is the creator of the popular web site **www.inspiration-for-singles.com**, which regularly receives visitors from more than 180 countries.

Jack is also the author of the ebooks **Outsmarting Loneliness, Single & Sure**, and **How to Master Your Money**. In the 1970s and 1980s, he authored four paperback western novels: **Rebel Town, The Wolfer, Penwhistle's Prize**, and **West of the Pecos**.

He holds bachelor's and master's degrees from Illinois State University. He has worked as a newspaper reporter, technical editor for the U.S. Department of Defense, publications manager for a utility company, and communications director for a national nonprofit organization.

"As someone who has never been married, I think I have a more accurate perspective on the single life than pastors or writers who have been married most of their life," Jack says. "I don't agree with those ministers who say 'Jesus can meet all your needs.' Jesus himself, while he was on earth, learned firsthand that human beings need the love and friendship of other people. He got lonely, just as we do, so that proves it's part of the human condition."

Both in his ebooks and on his web site, Jack tries to approach the problems of singleness in a practical way. A lifelong Christian, he firmly believes we cannot live the

Christian life--or the single life--without the constant help of God.

Jack lives in Illinois, USA.

Books You'll Want to Read

~~~~~
=====

These books made a major impact on my life as I was searching for truth and spiritual maturity. I can wholeheartedly recommend each one. They're available free at your public library through interlibrary loan or from online booksellers:

Arise from Darkness: What to Do When Life Doesn't Make Sense
Benedict J. Groeschel

Depression: A Stubborn Darkness
Edward T. Welch

Feeling Good: The New Mood Therapy
David D. Burns

Happiness Is a Choice: The Symptoms, Causes, and Cures of Depression
Frank M.D. Minirth and Dr. Paul Meier

Heaven
Randy Alcorn

How to Stop Worrying and Start Living
Dale Carnegie

Life Application Study Bible
available in NIV, NLT, KJV, NKJV, NASB, and Large Print
Editions

Man's Search for Meaning
Victor Frankl

The Search for Significance
Robert S. McGee

The Single Truth
Lori Smith

You Just Don't Understand: Women and Men in Conversation
Deborah Tannen

Kindle ebooks by Jack Zavada

Outsmarting Loneliness

Novels

Christmas Romance 3-Pack

Mr. Lincoln for the Defense

Killers on My Trail

For more on the single life, visit Jack Zavada's web site: www.inspiration-for-singles.com.

67576587R00113

Made in the USA
Lexington, KY
16 September 2017